BUSINESS MANAGERS

SECOND EDITION

Ferguson
An imprint of Infobase Publishing

Ferguson
An imprint of Infobase Publishing
132 West 31st Street
New York NY 10001

Library of Congress Cataloging-in-Publication Data

Careers in focus. Business managers. — 2nd ed.
    p. cm.
    Includes bibliographical references and index.
    ISBN-13: 978-0-8160-7296-5 (alk. paper)
    ISBN-10: 0-8160-7296-5 (alk. paper)
    1. Executives—Vocational guidance—United States—Juvenile literature. 2. Career development—United States—Juvenile literature. 3. Executive ability—United States—Juvenile literature. [1. Executives—Vocational guidance. 2. Management—Vocational guidance. 3. Vocational guidance.] I. Ferguson Publishing.
    HD38.25.U6C3675 2008
    658.40023'73—dc22
                                        2008032973

Ferguson books are available at special discounts when purchased in bulk quantities for businesses, associations, institutions, or sales promotions. Please call our Special Sales Department in New York at (212) 967-8800 or (800) 322-8755.

You can find Ferguson on the World Wide Web at http://www.fergpubco.com

Text design by David Strelecky
Cover design by Salvatore Luongo

Printed in the United States of America

MP MSRF 10 9 8 7 6 5 4 3 2 1

This book is printed on acid-free paper.

Table of Contents

Introduction

All businesses can be defined as organizations that provide customers with the goods and services they want. Most businesses attempt to make a profit. That is, to make more money than it takes to run the business. Some businesses, however, attempt only to make enough money to cover their operating expenses. These businesses, which are often social service agencies, hospitals, foundations, or advocacy groups, are called nonprofits or not-for-profits.

Management is found in every industry, including the industries of food, clothing, banking, education, health care, Information Technology, and business services. All types of businesses hire managers to formulate policies and administer the firm's operations. Managers may oversee the operations of an entire company, a geographical territory of a company's operations, or a specific department such as sales and marketing.

If a business is privately owned, the owner may be the manager. In a large corporation, however, there will be a management structure above the business manager.

Because it is such a broad category, it is difficult to project growth for business as a whole. It is entirely possible, and even common, for one industry to suffer slow growth or decline, while another industry thrives. There are certain trends, however, that may affect business as a whole.

One such trend is the increased use of technology. Internet Executives and Internet Store Managers and Entrepreneurs are building successful careers as computers and the World Wide Web become essential for more and more businesses. Many business managers are greatly affected by changes in the economy, especially Property and Real Estate Managers, Restaurant and Food Service Managers, and Retail Business Owners.

Workers with the most potential in this field are those who have strong leadership skills, seek further training or education, and are always aware that changing technology and a global economy will affect jobs and opportunities in their industry.

Each article in this book discusses in detail a particular business manager occupation. The articles in *Careers in Focus: Business Managers* appear in Ferguson's *Encyclopedia of Careers and Vocational Guidance,* but have been updated and revised with the latest information from the U.S. Department of Labor, professional organizations, and other sources.

The following paragraphs detail the sections and features that appear in the book.

The **Quick Facts** section provides a brief summary of the career including recommended school subjects, personal skills, work environment, minimum educational requirements, salary ranges, certification or licensing requirements, and employment outlook. This section also provides acronyms and identification numbers for the following government classification indexes: the Dictionary of Occupational Titles (DOT), the Guide for Occupational Exploration (GOE), the National Occupational Classification (NOC) Index, and the Occupational Information Network (O*NET)-Standard Occupational Classification System (SOC) index. The DOT, GOE, and O*NET-SOC indexes have been created by the U.S. government; the NOC index is Canada's career classification system. Readers can use the identification numbers listed in the Quick Facts section to access further information about a career. Print editions of the DOT (*Dictionary of Occupational Titles*. Indianapolis, Ind.: JIST Works, 1991) and GOE (*Guide for Occupational Exploration*. Indianapolis, Ind.: JIST Works, 2001) are available at libraries. Electronic versions of the NOC (http://www23.hrdc-drhc.gc.ca) and O*NET-SOC (http://online.onetcenter.org) are available on the Internet. When no DOT, GOE, NOC, or O*NET-SOC numbers are present, this means that the U.S. Department of Labor or Human Resources Development Canada have not created a numerical designation for this career. In this instance, you will see the acronym "N/A," or not available.

The **Overview** section is a brief introductory description of the duties and responsibilities involved in this career. Oftentimes, a career may have a variety of job titles. When this is the case, alternative career titles are presented. Employment statistics are also provided, when available. The **History** section describes the history of the particular job as it relates to the overall development of its industry or field. **The Job** describes the primary and secondary duties of the job. **Requirements** discusses high school and postsecondary education and training requirements, any certification or licensing that is necessary, and other personal requirements for success in the job. **Exploring** offers suggestions on how to gain experience in or knowledge of the particular job before making a firm educational and financial commitment. The focus is on what can be done while still in high school (or in the early years of college) to gain a better understanding of the job. The **Employers** section gives an overview of typical places of employment for the job. **Starting Out** discusses the best ways to land that first job, be it through the college career services office, newspaper ads, Internet employment sites, or personal contact. The **Advancement** section describes what kind of career path to expect from the job and how to get there. **Earnings** lists salary ranges and describes the typical fringe benefits. The **Work Environment** section describes the typical surroundings and conditions of employment—whether indoors or outdoors, noisy or quiet, social or independent. Also discussed are typical hours worked, any seasonal fluctuations, and the stresses and strains of the job. The **Outlook** section summarizes the job in terms of the general economy and industry projections. For the most part, Outlook information is obtained from the U.S. Bureau of Labor Statistics and is supplemented by information gathered from professional associations. Job growth terms follow those used in the *Occupational Outlook Handbook*. Growth described as "much faster than the average" means an increase of 21 percent or more. Growth described as "faster than the average" means an increase of 14 to 20 percent. Growth described as "about as fast as the average" means an increase of 7 to 13 percent. Growth described as "more slowly than the average" means an increase of 3 to 6 percent. "Little or no change" means a decrease of 2 percent to an increase of 2 percent. "Decline" means a decrease of 3 percent or more. Each article ends with **For More Information,** which lists organizations that provide information on training, education, internships, scholarships, and job placement.

Careers in Focus: Business Managers also includes photographs, informative sidebars, and interviews with professionals in the field.

Business Managers

OVERVIEW

Business managers plan, organize, direct, and coordinate the operations of firms in business and industry. They may oversee an entire company, a geographical territory of a company's operations, or a specific department within a company. Of the approximately 2.2 million managerial jobs in the United States, about 75 percent are found in service-providing industries (including the government).

HISTORY

Everyone has some experience in management. For example, if you schedule your day so that you can get up, get to school on time, go to soccer practice after school, have the time to do your homework, and get to bed at a reasonable hour, you are practicing management skills. Running a household, paying bills, balancing a checkbook, and keeping track of appointments, meetings, and social activities are also examples of managerial activities. Essentially, the term "manage" means to handle, direct, or control.

Management is a necessary part of any enterprise in which a person or group of people are trying to accomplish a specific goal. In fact, civilization could not have grown to its present level of complexity without the planning and organizing involved in effective management. Some of the earliest examples of written documents had to do with the management of business and commerce. As societies and individuals accumulated property and wealth, they needed effective record keeping of taxes, trade agreements, laws, and rights of ownership.

QUICK FACTS

School Subjects
Business
Computer science
Economics

Personal Skills
Helping/teaching
Leadership/management

Work Environment
Primarily indoors
One location with some
travel

Minimum Education Level
Bachelor's degree

Salary Range
$42,000 to $85,230 to
$185,540+

Certification or Licensing
None available

Outlook
Little or no change

DOT
189

GOE
09.01.01, 10.01.01, 13.01.01

NOC
0611

O*NET-SOC
11-1011.00, 11-1011.02,
11-1021.00, 11-3031.01

The technological advances of the Industrial Revolution brought about the need for a distinct class of managers. As complex factory systems developed, skilled and trained managers were required to organize and operate them. Workers became specialized in a limited number of tasks, which required managers to coordinate and oversee production.

As businesses began to diversify their production, industries became so complex that their management had to be divided among several different managers, as opposed to one central, authoritarian manager. With the expanded scope of managers and the trend toward decentralized management, the transition to the professional manager took place. In the 1920s, large corporations began to organize with decentralized administration and centralized policy control.

Managers provided a forum for the exchange and evaluation of creative ideas and technical innovations. Eventually these management concepts spread from manufacturing and production to office, personnel, marketing, and financial functions. Today, management is more concerned with results than activities, taking into account individual differences in styles of working.

THE JOB

Management is found in every industry, including food, clothing, banking, education, health care, and business services. All types of businesses have managers to formulate policies and administer the firm's operations. Managers may oversee the operations of an entire company, a geographical territory of a company's operations, or a specific department, such as sales and marketing.

Business managers direct a company's or a department's daily activities within the context of the organization's overall plan. They implement organizational policies and goals. This may involve developing sales or promotional materials, analyzing the department's budgetary requirements, and hiring, training, and supervising staff. Business managers are often responsible for long-range planning for their company or department. This involves setting goals for the organization and developing a workable plan for meeting those goals.

A manager responsible for a single department might work to coordinate his or her department's activities with other departments. A manager responsible for an entire company or organization might work with the managers of various departments or locations to oversee and coordinate the activities of all departments. If the business is privately owned, the owner may be the manager. In a large corporation, however, there will be a management structure above the business manager.

Jeff Bowe is the Midwest general manager for Disc Graphics, a large printing company headquartered in New York. Bowe oversees all aspects of the company's Indianapolis plant, which employs about 50 people. When asked what he is responsible for, Bowe answers, "Everything that happens in this facility." Specifically, that includes sales, production, customer service, capital expenditure planning, hiring and training employees, firing or downsizing, and personnel management.

The hierarchy of managers includes top executives, such as the president, who establishes an organization's goals and policies along with others, such as the chief executive officer, chief financial officer, chief information officer, executive vice president, and the board of directors. Top executives plan business objectives and develop policies to coordinate operations between divisions and departments and establish procedures for attaining objectives. Activity reports and financial statements are reviewed to determine progress and revise operations as needed. The president also directs and formulates funding for new and existing programs within the organization. Public relations plays a big part in the lives of executives as they deal with executives and leaders from other countries or organizations, and with customers, employees, and various special interest groups.

The top-level managers for Bowe's company are located in the company's New York headquarters. Bowe is responsible for reporting certain information about the Indianapolis facility to them. He may also have to work collaboratively with them on certain projects or plans. "I have a conversation with people at headquarters about every two to three days." he says. "I get corporate input on very large projects. I would also work closely with them if we had some type of corporate-wide program we were working on—something where I would be the contact person for this facility."

Although the president or chief executive officer retains ultimate authority and responsibility, Bowe is responsible for overseeing the day-to-day operations of the Indianapolis location. A manager in this position is sometimes called a *chief operating officer* or *COO*. Other duties of a COO may include serving as chair of committees, such as management, executive, engineering, or sales.

Some companies have an *executive vice president,* who directs and coordinates the activities of one or more departments, depending on the size of the organization. In very large organizations, the duties of executive vice presidents may be highly specialized. For example, they may oversee the activities of business managers of marketing, sales promotion, purchasing, finance, personnel training, industrial relations, administrative services, data processing, property management, transportation, or legal services. In smaller organizations, an executive vice president might be responsible for a number of these departments. Executive vice presidents also assist the chief executive officer in formulating and administering the organization's policies and developing its long-range goals. Executive vice presidents may serve as members of management committees on special studies.

Companies may also have a *chief financial officer* or *CFO*. In small firms, the CFO is usually responsible for all financial management tasks, such as budgeting, capital expenditure planning, cash flow, and various financial reviews and reports. In larger companies, the CFO may oversee financial management departments, to help other managers develop financial and economic policy and oversee the implementation of these policies.

Chief information officers, or *CIOs,* are responsible for all aspects of their company's information technology. They use their knowledge of technology and business to determine how information technology can best be used to meet company goals. This may include researching, purchasing, and overseeing the set up and use of technology systems, such as Intranet, Internet, and computer networks. These managers sometimes take a role in implementing a company's Web site. For more information on this career, see the article Chief Information Officers.

In companies that have several different locations, managers may be assigned to oversee specific geographic areas. For example, a large retailer with facilities all across the nation is likely to have a number of managers in charge of various territories. There might be a Midwest manager, a Southwest manager, a Southeast manager, a Northeast manager, and a Northwest manager. These managers are often called *regional* or *area managers.* Some companies break their management territories up into even smaller sections, such as a single state or a part of a state. Managers overseeing these smaller segments are often called *district managers,* and typically report directly to an area or regional manager.

REQUIREMENTS

High School

The educational background of business managers varies as widely as the nature of their diverse responsibilities. Many have a bachelor's degree in liberal arts or business administration. If you are interested in a business managerial career, you should start preparing in high school by taking college preparatory classes. According to

Jeff Bowe, your best bet academically is to get a well-rounded education. Because communication is important, take as many English classes as possible. Speech classes are another way to improve your communication skills. Courses in mathematics, business, and computer science are also excellent choices to help you prepare for this career. Finally, Bowe recommends taking a foreign language. "Today speaking a foreign language is more and more important," he says. "Which language is not so important. Any of the global languages are something you could very well use, depending upon where you end up."

Postsecondary Training

Business managers often have a college degree in a subject that pertains to the department they direct or the organization they administer; for example, accounting or economics for a business manager of finance, computer science for a business manager of data processing, engineering or science for a director of research and development. As computer usage grows, many managers are expected to have experience with the information technology that applies to their field.

Graduate and professional degrees are common. Bowe, along with many managers in administrative, marketing, financial, and manufacturing activities, has a master's degree in business administration. Managers in highly technical manufacturing and research activities often have a master's degree or doctorate in a technical or scientific discipline. A law degree is mandatory for business managers of corporate legal departments, and hospital managers generally have a master's degree in health services administration or business administration. In some industries, such as retail trade or the food and beverage industry, competent individuals without a college degree may become business managers.

Other Requirements

There are a number of personal characteristics that help one be a successful business manager, depending upon the specific responsibilities of the position. A manager who oversees other employees should have good communication and interpersonal skills. The ability to delegate work is another important personality trait of a good manager. The ability to think on your feet is often key in business management, according to Bowe. "You have to be able to think extremely quickly and not in a reactionary manner," he says. Bowe also says that a certain degree of organization is important, since managers often manage several different tasks simultaneously. Other traits considered important for top executives are intelligence, decisiveness, intuition, creativity, honesty, loyalty, a sense of responsibility, and planning abilities. Finally, the successful manager should be flexible and interested in staying abreast of new developments in his or her industry. "In general, you need to be open to change because your customers change, your market changes, your technology changes," he says. "If you won't try something new, you really have no business being in management."

EXPLORING

To get experience as a manager, start with your own interests. Whether you're involved in drama, sports, school publications, or a part-time job, there are managerial duties associated with any organized activity. These can involve planning, scheduling, managing other workers or volunteers, fund-raising, or budgeting. Local businesses also have job opportunities through which you can get firsthand knowledge and experience of management structure. If you can't get an actual job, at least try to schedule a meeting with a business manager to talk with him or her about the career. Some schools or community organizations arrange job-shadowing, where you can spend part of a day "shadowing" a selected employee to see what his or her job is like. Joining Junior Achievement (http://www.ja.org) is another excellent way to get involved with local businesses and learn about how they work. Finally, take every opportunity to work with computers, since computer skills are vital to today's business world.

EMPLOYERS

There are approximately 2.2 million general and operations managers and executives employed in the United States. These jobs are found in every industry. However, approximately 75 percent work in service industries.

Virtually every business in the United States has some form of managerial positions. Obviously, the larger the company is, the more managerial positions it is likely to have. Another factor is the geographical territory covered by the business. It is safe to say that companies doing business in larger geographical territories are likely to have more managerial positions than those with smaller territories.

STARTING OUT

Generally, you will need a college degree, although many retail stores, grocery stores, and restaurants hire promising applicants who have only a high school diploma. Job seekers usually apply directly to the manager of such places. Your college career services office is often the best place to start looking for these positions. A number of listings can also be found in newspaper help wanted ads.

Many organizations have management trainee programs that college graduates can enter. Such programs are advertised at college career fairs or through college job placement services. Often, however, these management trainee positions in business and government are filled by employees who are already working for the organization and who demonstrate management potential. Jeff Bowe suggests researching the industry you are interested in to find out what might be the best point of entry for that field. "I came into the printing company through customer service, which is a good point of entry because it's one of the easiest things to learn," he says. "Although it requires more technical know-how now than it did then, customer service is still not a bad entry point for this industry."

ADVANCEMENT

Most business management and top executive positions are filled by experienced lower-level managers and executives who display valuable managerial traits, such as leadership, self-confidence, creativity, motivation, decisiveness, and flexibility. In small firms, advancement to a higher management position may come slowly, while promotions may occur more quickly in larger firms.

Advancement may be accelerated by participating in different kinds of educational programs available for managers. These are often paid for by the organization. Company training programs broaden knowledge of company policy and operations. Training programs sponsored by industry and trade associations and continuing education courses in colleges and universities can familiarize managers with the latest developments in management techniques. In recent years, large numbers of middle managers were laid off as companies streamlined operations. Competition for jobs is keen, and business managers committed to improving their knowledge of the field and of related disciplines—especially computer information systems—will have the best opportunities for advancement.

Business managers may advance to executive or administrative vice president. Vice presidents may advance to peak corporate positions—president or chief executive officer. Presidents and chief executive officers, upon retirement, may become members of the board of directors of one or more firms. Sometimes business managers establish their own firms.

EARNINGS

Salary levels for business managers vary substantially, depending upon the level of responsibility, length of service, and type, size, and location of the organization. Top-level managers in large firms can earn much more than their counterparts in small firms. Salaries in large metropolitan areas, such as New York City, are higher than those in smaller cities.

According to the U.S. Department of Labor, general and operations managers had a median yearly income of $85,230 in 2006. The lowest 10 percent of this group earned approximately $42,000 annually. To show the range of earnings for general and operations managers, however, the department notes that those in the computer and peripheral equipment manufacturing industry had annual mean earnings of $139,800; those in architectural, engineering, and related services, $120,620; and those employed in local government, $79,130.

Chief executives earned a mean salary of $144,600 annually in 2006, according to the U.S. Department of Labor. Similarly, salaries varied by industry. For example, the mean yearly salary for those involved in the management of companies and enterprises was $166,010, while those employed by financial investment firms earned a mean salary of $185,540. The business publication *The NonProfit Times*, which conducts periodic salary surveys, reports the average earnings for CEOs and executive directors at nonprofit social services and welfare organizations were approximately $100,118 in 2006. Some executives, however, earn hundreds of thousands of dollars more than this annually.

Benefit and compensation packages for business managers are usually excellent, and may even include such things as bonuses, stock awards, company-paid insurance premiums, use of company cars, paid country club memberships, expense accounts, and generous retirement benefits.

WORK ENVIRONMENT

Business managers are provided with comfortable offices near the departments they direct. Top executives may have spacious, lavish offices and may enjoy such privileges as executive dining rooms, company cars, country club memberships, and liberal expense accounts.

Managers often travel between national, regional, and local offices. Top executives may travel to meet with executives in other corporations, both within the United States and abroad. Meetings and conferences sponsored by industries and associations occur regularly and provide invaluable opportunities to meet with peers and keep up with the latest developments. In large corporations, job transfers between the parent company and its local offices or subsidiaries are common.

Business managers often work long hours under intense pressure to meet, for example, production and marketing goals. Jeff Bowe's average workweek consists of 55 to 60 hours at the office. This is not uncommon—in fact, some executive spend up to 80 hours working each week. These long hours limit time available for family and leisure activities.

OUTLOOK

Overall, employment of business managers and executives is expected to experience little or no growth through 2016, according to the U.S. Department of Labor. Many job openings will be the result of managers being promoted to better positions, retiring, or leaving their positions to start their own businesses. Even so, the compensation and prestige of these positions make them highly sought-after, and competition to fill openings will be intense.

Projected employment growth varies by industry. For example, employment in the professional, scientific, and technical services industry should increase faster than the average, while employment in some manufacturing industries is expected to decline.

The outlook for business managers is closely tied to the overall economy. When the economy is good, businesses expand both in terms of their output and the number of people they employ, which creates a need for more managers. In economic downturns, businesses often lay off employees and cut back on production, which lessens the need for managers.

Business managers who have knowledge of one or more foreign languages (such as Spanish or Mandarin) and experience in marketing, international economics, and information systems will have the best employment opportunities.

FOR MORE INFORMATION

For news about management trends, resources on career information and finding a job, and an online job bank, contact
American Management Association
1601 Broadway
New York, NY 10019-7434
Tel: 877-566-9441
http://www.amanet.org

For information about programs for students in kindergarten through high school, and information on local chapters, contact
Junior Achievement
One Education Way
Colorado Springs, CO 80906-4477
Tel: 719-540-8000
Email: newmedia@ja.org
http://www.ja.org

For information on management careers, contact
National Management Association
2210 Arbor Boulevard
Dayton, OH 45439-1506
Tel: 937-294-0421
Email: nma@nma1.org
http://nma1.org

Chief Information Officers

OVERVIEW

Chief information officers (CIOs), also known as information systems directors, are responsible for all aspects of their company's information technology. They use their knowledge of technology and business to determine how information technology can best be used to meet company goals. This may include researching, purchasing, and overseeing set-up and use of technology systems, such as intranet, Internet, and computer networks. These managers sometimes take a role in implementing a company's Web site. CIOs work for a variety of employers, including businesses, government agencies, libraries, and colleges and universities.

HISTORY

Over the past few decades, the importance of computer technology and the Internet has increased rapidly. The Internet, which did not exist in its current form until 1983, is now an integral part of nearly all business. It allows companies to conduct transactions in a matter of seconds, and people all over the world now rely on the World Wide Web as a quick resource on everything from education and current events to shopping and the stock market.

Because of this boom in the use and importance of computers and the Internet, workers must constantly be updated about changes in technology. It is the job of the chief information officer to make sure that all technology runs smoothly in an office, and that no workers are in the dark when it comes to

QUICK FACTS

School Subjects
Business
Computer science
English

Personal Skills
Helping/teaching
Leadership/management

Work Environment
Primarily indoors
One location with some
  travel

Minimum Education Level
Bachelor's degree

Salary Range
$40,000 to $144,600 to
  $183,450+

Certification or Licensing
None available

Outlook
Little or no change

DOT
189

GOE
09.01.01, 10.01.01, 13.01.01

NOC
0611

O*NET-SOC
11-1011.00

the company's computer systems. The position of chief information officer, though a relatively new job title, has quickly risen in importance and prestige and is firmly established among the top executive positions available in the business world.

THE JOB

Anyone who has read Scott Adams's comic strip Dilbert knows something about the imaginary wall between business executives and technology experts in the corporate world. On one side of the wall (so the Dilbert story goes), there are the folks who wear business suits and who don't know a laptop from an Etch-A-Sketch. On the other side of the wall, there are the geeks in tennis shoes who hang out in *Battlestar Galactica* chat rooms and couldn't care less about the company's mission statement. If popular lore is to be believed, confusion, hostility, and poor business practices abound whenever these two groups try to join forces.

It's the job of the CIO to enter this ongoing battle and find a way to straddle the wall between business and technology. Although they're up to date on cutting-edge information technology, today's CIOs must know their way around the company's business as well as any other high-level manager. That means they attend strategy sessions and management meetings, in addition to meeting with computer professionals and other members of the technical staff. Using their combined business and technical knowledge, CIOs usually oversee the selection and implementation of their company's information systems—from email programs to corporation-wide intranets.

Making these decisions requires enough technical savvy to choose appropriate technology systems from an array of complex options. Decisions like these, though, also require a sophisticated sense of how information in a company circulates and how that information relates to business practices. Does the company's customer database need to connect to the World Wide Web? What security issues are created if that connection is established? Who needs to be able to access the most sensitive information, and who needs to be locked out? Answering these sorts of questions can take all of a CIO's mix of executive knowledge and technical expertise.

For Chuck Cooper, the director of information systems at a major public library, making these sorts of decisions also requires a good understanding of the financial situation of his organization. He must select systems for his library staff that fit their needs and the library's often-limited budget. At the same time, he must consider what the library may need five and even 10 years down the road, since a lack of vision now can mean more money and time spent later. After systems have been selected, Cooper must establish and oversee vendor relationships (contractual agreements between the library and companies that supply technical equipment). Evaluating potential vendor relationships for financial and technological advantages takes up a large part of the CIO's working hours.

For most CIOs, though, actually choosing and implementing technology systems is just the beginning. For example, Cooper spends much of his time getting employees enthusiastic and informing them about new computer technology. "I spend a lot of my time trying to convince people of the utility of new systems," he explains. "Library people are reality-oriented. They have to kick the tires." For Cooper, giving his employees a chance to "kick the tires" of new systems means organizing targeted, hands-on demonstration sessions. Once they have a chance to test-drive new programs themselves, employees often become excited about the new services they'll be able to provide to library patrons.

REQUIREMENTS

High School
If you are interested in this career, you should start preparing in high school by taking college preparatory classes. Take as many computer science, mathematics, business, and English classes as possible. Speech classes are another way to improve your communication skills.

Postsecondary Training
Becoming a CIO requires a solid technology background and solid business understanding. In general, companies require their executives to have at least a bachelor of arts or bachelor of science degree, and often a master's in business administration as well.

If you're interested in becoming a CIO, you should be sure that your college degree provides you with both business and computer skills. Some programs devoted to providing this sort of background have begun to spring up, such as those offered by the School of Information at the University of California, Berkeley (http://www.ischool. berkeley.edu/programs/overview). The School offers a master's and Ph.D. in information management and systems.

Other Requirements
Equally important to training, though, are the communication skills you'll need to sell your co-workers and staff on the information strategies that you build. "Writing and especially speaking are crucial in

this business," Chuck Cooper points out. "You are constantly presenting yourself and your work to others, and you need to be able to communicate well in order to succeed." English, writing, and speech classes should help you hone your verbal communication skills.

EXPLORING

The best way to explore this field while you are still in high school is by joining computer clubs at school and community centers and learning all you can about the Internet, networks, and computer security. You might also get a part-time job that includes computer work. This can help you get exposure to computer systems and learn how they are used in a business.

To get management experience, start with your own interests. There are managerial duties associated with almost every organized activity, from the drama club or theatrical productions to sports or school publications.

EMPLOYERS

Until fairly recently, CIOs were found primarily at large corporations that could afford another high-level executive salary. According to *Inc.* magazine, though, smaller companies are now beginning to see the value of having a dedicated information director. "At smaller companies, technology has often been placed too low in the organization," Chuck Cooper points out. Without executive decision-making power, technology professionals often found their recommendations given insufficient weight. While this sort of strategy might save money in the short-term, small companies have gradually discovered that they pay later when outdated systems must be upgraded or altered. In fact, even nonprofits and other less mainstream small businesses have begun to hire CIOs.

STARTING OUT

Since CIOs are high-level executives, people usually spend several years working in business administration or information management before they apply for jobs at the CIO level. Lower- and mid-level information management jobs usually involve specialization in a certain area. For example, middle-level systems management professionals in Chuck Cooper's department may run technology training programs, design and implement help desks, or oversee small database systems.

ADVANCEMENT

After they've proven themselves at lower-level information management jobs, these employees begin to manage larger units, such as the user support program or the larger library database system. Eventually, some of these employees may have the business experience and broad technical background required to apply for jobs at the CIO level.

Other CIOs may find work at the executive level after making what's known as a lateral move—a move from a position in one department to a position at the same level in another department. For example, successful business administration professionals might be able to move into an information systems department as a manager rather than an entry-level database administrator. However, they would still need to prove they had managed to gain the technical knowledge required to do the job.

EARNINGS

Earnings among CIOs vary substantially based on the type of business, the size of the employer, the executive's experience, and other such factors. *Computerworld* reports that chief information officers earned an average salary (including bonuses) of $179,236 in 2007. According to the U.S. Department of Labor, the median annual income for all top executives, which includes CIOs, was $144,600 in 2006, with the lowest 10 percent of executives earning approximately $40,000 annually. Fields in which executives had higher mean salaries included depository credit intermediation, with a salary of $152,230; ISPs (Internet Service Providers) and Web search portals, $181,960; and securities and commodity exchanges, $183,450. The business publication *The NonProfit Times*, which conducts periodic salary surveys, reports the average earnings for top executives at nonprofit social services and welfare organizations were approximately $100,118 in 2006. Even those working for nonprofits, however, can command extremely high salaries.

Benefits for CIOs depend on the employer but generally include health insurance, retirement plans, and paid vacation and sick days. Bonuses and stock options may also be offered.

WORK ENVIRONMENT

The best part of being a CIO for Chuck Cooper comes when new technology is actually put in place. "When you see the effect of probably a year of planning, and it has a positive impact on the way the public uses the library, that's a nice feeling," he remarks. Especially because CIOs often spend time thinking about changes several years down the road, having a program actually "hit the streets," as Cooper puts it, is gratifying, especially when it allows library patrons and staff to access information in a way they never could before.

Although the payoff can be gratifying, the planning may not be, Cooper admits. "There's a lot of frustration caused by dead ends," he explains. "There are often projects that you try to get started that are dependent on other people, and you may have to wait or start over." The interdependence between technology and other library areas means that Cooper often spends years revising plans before they can get the go-ahead. The need to take strategies back to the drawing board can be the worst part of Cooper's work.

OUTLOOK

According to the U.S. Department of Labor, top executives, including CIOs, should experience little or no employment growth through 2016. As consumers and industries increasingly rely on computers and information technology, the expertise of CIOs will be in continuous demand. As computer technology becomes more sophisticated and more complex, corporations will increasingly require Information Science (IS) professionals capable of choosing among the ever-growing array of information technology options. Additionally, as small organizations begin to prioritize information management, more jobs should be available for CIOs outside of large corporations. Because some of these jobs are likely to be at nonprofit and educational institutions, IS professionals may have wider options when choosing an employer. Although salaries can be expected to be lower at these sorts of organizations, they may provide interested employees with a less formal and more service-oriented atmosphere.

FOR MORE INFORMATION

For information on careers, contact
Information Technology Association of America
1401 Wilson Boulevard, Suite 1100
Arlington, VA 22209-2318
Tel: 703-522-5055
http://www.itaa.org

For information about programs for students in kindergarten through high school, and information on local chapters, contact
Junior Achievement
One Education Way
Colorado Springs, CO 80906-4477
Tel: 719-540-8000
Email: newmedia@ja.org
http://www.ja.org

Financial Institution Officers and Managers

QUICK FACTS

School Subjects
Business
Mathematics

Personal Skills
Communication/ideas
Leadership/management

Work Environment
Primarily indoors
Primarily one location

Minimum Education Level
Bachelor's degree

Salary Range
$50,290 to $90,970 to
$125,180+

Certification or Licensing
Recommended

Outlook
About as fast as the average

DOT
186

GOE
13.01.01, 13.02.04

NOC
0122

O*NET-SOC
11-3031.01, 11-3031.02,
13-2071.00, 13-2072.00

OVERVIEW

Financial institution officers and managers oversee the activities of banks and personal credit institutions such as credit unions and finance companies. These establishments serve businesses, government agencies, and individuals. They lend money, maintain savings, enable people and businesses to write checks or make online payments for goods and services, rent safe-deposit boxes for storing valuables, manage trust funds, advise clients on investments and business affairs, issue credit cards and traveler's checks, and take payments for gas and electric bills. There are approximately 506,000 financial managers (including those working outside of financial institutions) employed in the United States.

HISTORY

The modern concept of bank notes, or currency, developed in the 17th century. Goldsmiths in London began to issue paper receipts for gold and other valuables that were deposited in their warehouses. The paper money we use today is a modern version of these 17th-century receipts.

The first bank in the United States, Bank of North America, was chartered by the Continental Congress in 1781. By the early 1900s, banks had become so numerous that federal control of banks was needed. The Federal Deposit System, as we know it today, is the result of the efforts to coordinate the activities of the many banks throughout the nation. As banks grew in number and competed to attract new customers, financial professionals developed a variety of new services for banks to offer. Advancements in technology made many of these new services possible and, often, changed the way people thought about money. For example, banks introduced the first credit cards that were accepted by multiple vendors (cards that we know as Visa, MasterCard, etc.) in the late 1950s and 1960s. The introduction of these credit cards was made possible by bank computers that were able to track transactions and signal when spending limits were reached. Today, credit cards have become so commonplace that CardWeb.com estimates that there are approximately 6,000 credit card issuers. The average American has eight credit cards and the average debt per household is $9,659 on all cards.

The banking industry continues to use technology to expand its services. Today, most major banks offer online banking. Other smaller banks at least have a presence on the Web. It is estimated that more than 28 million U.S. households bank online, and this number is expected to increase in the future.

Within the past 25 years, the number of banks and other financial institutions—as well as banking options—have grown extensively, and many financial professionals are needed to help run the banking industry.

THE JOB

Financial institutions include commercial banks, which provide full banking service for business, government, and individuals; investment banks, which offer their clients financial counseling and brokering; Federal Reserve Banks, whose customers are affiliated banks in their districts; or other organizations such as credit unions and finance companies.

These institutions employ many officers and managers whose duties vary depending on the type and size of the firm as well as on their own area of responsibility. All financial institutions operate under the direction of a president, who is guided by policies set by the board of directors. Vice presidents are department heads who are sometimes also responsible for certain key clients. Controllers handle bank funds, properties, and equipment. Large institutions may also have treasurers, loan officers, and officers in charge of departments such as trust, credit, and investment. A number of these positions are described in more detail in the following paragraphs.

The *financial institution president* directs the overall activities of the bank or consumer credit organization, making sure that its objectives are achieved without violating government regulations or overlooking any legal requirements. The officers are responsible for earning as much of a return as possible on the institution's investments within the restrictions demanded by government and sound business practices. They help set policies pertaining to investments, loans, interest, and reserves. They coordinate the activities of the various divisions and delegate authority to subordinate officers, who administer the operation of their own areas of responsibility. Financial institution presidents study financial reports and other data to keep up with changes in the economy that may affect their firm's policies.

The *vice president* coordinates many of the operations of the institution. This person is responsible for the activities of a regional bank office, branch bank, and often an administrative bank division or department. As designated by the board of directors, the vice president supervises programs such as installment loan, foreign trade, customer service, trust, and investment. The vice president also prepares studies for management and planning, like workload and budget estimates and activity and analysis reports.

The *administrative secretary* usually writes directions for supervisory workers that outline and explain policy. The administrative secretary acts, in effect, as an intermediary between minor supervisory workers and the executive officers.

The *financial institution treasurer* directs the bank's monetary programs, transactions, and security measures in accordance with banking principles and legislation. Treasurers coordinate program activity and evaluate operating practices to ensure efficient operations. They oversee receipt, disbursement, and expenditure of money, and sign documents approving or affecting monetary transactions. They direct the safekeeping and control of assets and securities and maintain specified legal cash reserves. They review financial and operating statements and present reports and recommendations to bank officials or board committees.

Controllers authorize the use of funds kept by the treasurer. They also supervise the maintenance of accounts and records, and analyze these records so that the directors or other bank officials will know how much the bank is spending for salaries, operating expenses, and other expenses. Controllers often formulate financial policies.

The *financial institution manager* establishes and maintains relationships with the community. This person's responsibility is to supervise accounting and reporting functions and to establish operating policies and procedures. The manager directs several activities within the bank. The assets, records, collateral, and securities held by the financial institution are in the manager's custody. Managers approve loans of various types, such as credit, commercial, real estate, and consumer loans. They also direct personnel in trust activities.

The *loan officer* and the *credit and collection manager* both deal with customers who are seeking or have obtained loans or credit. The loan officer specializes in examining and evaluating applications for lines of credit, installment credit, or commercial, real estate, and consumer loans and has the authority to approve them within a specified limit or recommend their approval to the loan committee. To determine the feasibility of granting a loan request, the officer analyzes the applicant's financial status, credit, and property evaluation. The job may also include handling foreclosure proceedings. Depending on training and experience, officers may analyze potential loan markets to develop prospects for loans. They negotiate the terms of transaction and draw up the requisite documents to buy and sell contracts, loans, or real estate. Credit and collection managers draw up collection notices for customers who already have credit. When the bank has difficulty collecting accounts or receives a worthless check, credit and collection managers take steps to correct the situation. Managers must keep records of all credit and collection transactions.

Loan counselors study the records of the account when payments on a loan are overdue and contact the borrower to discuss payment of the loan. They may analyze the borrower's financial problems and make new arrangements for repayment of the loan. If a loan account is uncollectible, they prepare a report for the bank or institution's files.

Credit card operations managers are responsible for the overall credit card policies and operations of a bank, commercial establishment, or credit card company. They establish procedures for verifying the information on application forms, determine applicants' credit worthiness, approve the issuance of credit cards, and set a credit limit on each account. These managers coordinate the work involved with reviewing unpaid balances, collecting delinquent accounts, investigating and preventing fraud, voiding lost or stolen credit cards, keeping records, and exchanging information with the company's branches and other credit card companies.

The *letter of credit negotiator* works with clients who hold letters of credit used in international banking. This person contacts foreign banks, suppliers, and other sources to obtain documents needed to authorize the requested loan. Then the negotiator checks to see if the documents have been completed correctly so that the conditions set forth in the letter of credit meet with policy and code requirements. Before authorizing payment, the negotiator verifies the client's credit rating and may request increasing the collateral or reducing the amount of purchases, amending the contract accordingly. The letter of credit negotiator specifies the method of payment and informs the foreign bank when a loan has gone unpaid for a certain length of time.

The *trust officer* directs operations concerning the administration of private, corporate, and probate trusts. Officers examine or draft trust agreements to ensure compliance with legal requirements and terms creating trusts. They locate, inventory, and evaluate assets of probated accounts. They also direct realization of assets, liquidation of liabilities, payment of bills, preparation of federal and state tax returns on trust income, and collection of earnings. They represent the institution in trust fund negotiations.

Reserve officers maintain the institution's reserve funds according to policy and as required by law. They regulate the flow of money through branches, correspondent banks, and the Federal Reserve Bank. They also consolidate financial statements, calculate the legal reserve, and compile statistical and analytical reports of the reserves.

Foreign-exchange traders maintain the balance that the institution has on deposit in foreign banks to ensure its foreign-exchange position and determine the prices at which that exchange will be purchased and sold. Their conclusions are based on an analysis of demand, supply, and the stability of the currency. They establish local rates of exchange based upon money market quotations or the customer's financial standing. They also buy and sell foreign-exchange drafts and compute the proceeds.

The *securities trader* performs securities investment and counseling service for the bank and its customers. They study financial background and future trends and advise financial institution officers and customers regarding investments in stocks and bonds. They transmit buy-and-sell orders to a trading desk or broker as directed and recommend purchase, retention, or sale of issues. They compute extensions, commissions, and other charges for billing customers and making payments for securities.

The *operations officer* is in charge of the internal operations in a department or branch office of a financial institution. This person is responsible for the smooth and efficient operation of a particular area. Duties include interviewing, hiring, and directing the training of employees, as well as supervising their activities, evaluating their performance, and making certain that they comply with established procedures. Operations officers audit accounts, records, and certifications and verify the count of incoming cash. They prepare reports on the activities of the department or branch, control the supply of money for its needs, and perform other managerial tasks of a general nature.

Facts About the Banking Industry

- The first bank in the United States, Bank of North America, was chartered by the Continental Congress in 1781.
- There are more than 94,000 bank offices and branches in the United States.
- The first ATM (cash dispensing only) was introduced at the Chemical Bank, Long Island, New York, in 1969.
- The first multi-function ATM was introduced at Citizens & Southern National Bank in Atlanta, Georgia, in 1971.
- There were 396,000 ATMs in the United States and 10.5 billion ATM transactions in 2005.
- In 2004, 34 percent of Americans preferred to do their banking at a traditional branch, 24 percent at a drive-thru teller, 21 percent at a branch ATM, 17 percent online, and 4 percent at an in-store branch.
- Checks were first used in Holland in the early 1500s.
- Financial institutions process 36.7 billion checks annually.

Sources: American Bankers Association, Gallup Organization, *American Banker*

The *credit union manager* directs the operations of credit unions, which are chartered by the state or federal government to provide savings and loan services to their members. This manager reviews loan applications, arranges automatic payroll deductions for credit union members wishing to make regular savings deposits or loan payments, and assists in collecting delinquent accounts. Managers prepare financial statements, help the government audit credit union records, and supervise bookkeeping and clerical activities. Acting as a management representative of the credit union, credit union managers have the power to sign legal documents and checks on behalf of the board of directors. They also oversee control of the credit union's assets and advise the board on how to invest its funds.

REQUIREMENTS

High School

You will need at least a bachelor's degree if you want to work as a financial institution officer or manager. While you are in high school, therefore, you should take classes that will give you a solid preparation for college. These classes include mathematics, such as algebra and geometry, science, history, and a foreign language. Take English courses to improve your researching, writing, and communication skills. Also, take computer classes. Computer technology is an integral part of today's financial world, and you will benefit from being familiar with this tool. Finally, if your high school offers classes in economics, accounting, or finance, be sure to take these courses. The course work will not only give you an opportunity to gain knowledge but will also allow you to see if you enjoy working with numbers and theories.

Postsecondary Training

Possible college majors include accounting, economics, finance, or business administration with an emphasis on accounting or finance. You will need to continue honing your computer skills during this time. In addition, you will probably have exposure to business law classes. Federal and state laws regarding business and finances change, so you will need to familiarize yourself with current regulations.

Financial institutions increasingly seek candidates with master's degrees in business administration for positions as managers. So keep in mind that you may have to pursue further education even after you have completed your bachelor's degree. No matter what level of degree you obtain, however, you will also need to keep up your education even as you work. Many financial management and banking associations offer continuing education programs in conjunction with colleges or universities. These programs are geared toward advancing and updating your knowledge of subjects such as changing banking regulations, financial analysis, and international banking.

Certification or Licensing

Certification is one way to show your commitment to the field, improve your skills, and increase your possibilities for advancement. Professional certification is available in specialized fields such as investment and credit management. Requirements for earning the designation chartered financial analyst, which is conferred by the CFA Institute, include having the educational background to be able to do master's level work, passing three levels of tests, and having three or more years of experience in the field. The National Association of Credit Management offers business credit professionals a three-part certification program that consists of work experience and examinations. Financial managers pass through the level of credit business associate to credit business fellow to certified credit executive. The Association for Financial Professionals confers the certified treasury professional (formerly known as the certified cash manager) and the certified treasury professional associate designations. Applicants must pass an examination and have working experience in the field.

Other Requirements

In the banking business, the ability to get along well with others is essential. You should be able to show tact and convey a feeling of understanding and confidence. Honesty is perhaps the most important qualification for this job. These officers and managers handle large sums of money and have access to confidential financial information about the individuals and business concerns associated with their institutions. Therefore, if you are interested in this career, you must have a high degree of personal integrity.

EXPLORING

Except for high school courses that are business oriented, you will find few opportunities for experience and exploration during high school. Ask your teacher or guidance counselor to arrange a class tour of a financial institution. This will at least give you a taste of how banking services work. You can gain the most valuable experience by finding a part-time or a summer job in a bank or other institution that sometimes hires qualified high school or college students. Finally, to gain some hands-on experience with managing money, consider joining a school or local club in which you could work as the treasurer.

EMPLOYERS

Financial managers and related workers hold approximately 506,000 jobs. They primarily work for banks and personal credit institutions such as credit unions and finance companies.

STARTING OUT

One way to enter banking as a regular employee is through part-time or summer employment. Anyone can apply for a position by writing to a financial institution officer in charge of personnel or by arranging for an interview. Many institutions advertise in the classified section of local newspapers. The larger banks recruit on college campuses. An officer will visit a campus and conduct interviews at that time. Student career services offices can also arrange interviews.

ADVANCEMENT

There is no one method for advancement among financial institution officers. Advancement depends on the size of the institution, the services it offers, and the qualifications of the employee. Usually, smaller employers offer a slower rate of job advancement than larger employers.

Financial institutions often offer special training programs that take place at night, during the summer, and in some special instances during scheduled working hours. People who take advantage of these opportunities usually find that advancement comes more quickly. The American Banking Institute (part of the American Bankers Association), for example, offers training in every phase of banking through its own facilities or the facilities of local universities and banking organizations. The length of this training may vary from six months to two years. Years of service and experience are required for a top-level financial institution officer to become acquainted with policy, operations, customers, and the community. Similarly, the National Association of Credit Management offers training and instruction.

EARNINGS

Those who enter banking in the next few years will find their earnings to be dependent on their experience, the size of the institution, and its location. In general, starting salaries in financial institutions are not usually the highest, although among larger financial institutions in big cities, starting salaries often compare favorably with salaries in large corporations. After five to 10 years of experience, the salaries of officers usually are slightly higher than those in large corporations for people with comparable experience.

Financial managers earned a median annual salary of $90,970 in 2006, according to the U.S. Department of Labor. Also according to the department, the lowest paid 10 percent of financial managers made approximately $50,290, while the highest paid 25 percent earned $125,180 or more.

Group life insurance, paid vacations, profit-sharing plans, and health care and retirement plans are some of the benefits offered to financial officers and managers.

WORK ENVIRONMENT

Working conditions in financial institutions are generally pleasant. They are usually clean, well maintained, and often air-conditioned. They are generally located throughout cities for the convenience of both customers and employees. Working hours for financial institution officers and managers may be somewhat irregular, as many organizations have expanded their hours of business.

OUTLOOK

Employment for financial institution officers and managers is expected to increase about as fast as the average for all occupations through 2016, according to the U.S. Department of Labor. The need for skilled professionals will increase primarily as a result of greater domestic and foreign competition, changing laws affecting taxes and other financial matters, and a growing emphasis on accurate reporting of financial data for both financial institutions and corporations.

Competition for these jobs will be strong, however, for several reasons. Financial institution officers and managers are often promoted from within the ranks of the organization, and, once established in their jobs, they tend to stay for many years. In addition, more qualified applicants are becoming available each year to fill vacancies; workers who have earned a master's degree in business administration will enjoy the lowest unemployment rates. Chances for employment will be best for workers who are familiar with a range of financial services, such as banking, insurance, real estate, and securities, and for those experienced in computers and data processing systems.

FOR MORE INFORMATION

This organization has information about the banking industry and continuing education available through the American Institute of Banking. It also has information on the Stonier Graduate School of Banking.

American Bankers Association
1120 Connecticut Avenue, NW
Washington, DC 20036-3902
Tel: 800-226-5377
http://www.aba.com

For certification, industry news, and career information, contact
Association for Financial Professionals
4520 East West Highway, Suite 750
Bethesda, MD 20814-3574
Tel: 301-907-2862
http://www.afponline.org

For information on the chartered financial analyst designation, contact
CFA Institute
560 Ray C. Hunt Drive
Charlottesville, VA 22903-2981
Tel: 800-247-8132
Email: info@cfainstitute.org
http://www.cfainstitute.org

For information on certification, continuing education, and general information on the banking and credit industry, contact
National Association of Credit Management
8840 Columbia 100 Parkway
Columbia, MD 21045-2158
Tel: 410-740-5560
http://www.nacm.org

INTERVIEW

Denise Hearson is a branch manager/loan officer with Legacy Bank in Wichita, Kansas. She has worked in banking since 1996. Denise discussed her career with the editors of Careers in Focus: Business Managers.

Q. Why did you decide to enter this career?

A. When I started working at a bank, it was really just intended to be short-term over the summer. My background is actually in education. I graduated from college with a bachelor of arts in elementary education with an emphasis in middle school science. The year after graduating, I lived in very small towns with little educator turnover and substitute taught hoping to work my way into a school district full time. However, over the summer while school was not in session, I applied to work at a local bank. I loved banking so much that I never went back to teaching.

Q. After you were hired at the bank, how did you train for the field?

A. When I entered the banking field, I started at the bottom of the totem pole. I helped out in as many areas of the bank as I could, thus learning many aspects of banking. I helped answer phones, opened new accounts, and filled in as a teller as needed. Eventually, I became an administrative assistant to the president and started doing some of the legwork for his lending. I learned the process and became a lender myself. I also was in charge of implementing a computer network into the bank at the time. It was helpful to attend lending conferences that were presented by the state's banking association. I also took a couple of online classes related to finance and lending. I believe that if you find a field of work that you really enjoy, you can work hard to become more knowledgeable in that field through hands-on experience as well by attending as many trainings as your employer will allow.

Q. What are your primary and secondary job duties?

A. Currently, my duties are two-fold, with one not necessarily taking precedence over the other. I am responsible for maintaining the branch building and supervising all staff at my location (branch manager). I work with vendors and other bank management to make sure the building is maintained and secured properly. My staff of four employees is very independent and responsible for their duties, but I oversee their procedures and advise them as needed. I set schedules and hold meetings as necessary. My other duty is related to lending (loan officer). I work with customers to fulfill their loan requests and counsel them on their finances when I am unable to meet their requests.

Q. What do you like most and least about your job?

A. My favorite part of my job is lending. I enjoy being able to help customers meet their goals and reach their dreams. Whether it is helping a student buy their first car, a new couple buy their first home, or just helping out someone in a bind, it is enjoyable to share in their excitement. Of course, my least favorite part is collections. I try to make sound lending decisions to keep defaults to a minimum, but situations change in people's lives that make it difficult for them to keep up their end of the contract. Usually an agreement can be made between the borrower and myself. This allows the borrower to maintain their good credit and keep the loan in good standing.

Q. What advice would you give to high school students who are interested in becoming financial institution managers?

A. The activities available today are probably more diverse than when I went through school! Depending on what area of banking someone desires to go into, any activities related to improving communication skills and knowledge of computers, accounting, and finance would all be helpful. In many banks, sales are becoming a requirement of everyone that has contact with customers. Employees must be prepared to cross-sell or bring in new customers. We have many high school and college students who work at the bank during the summer and other breaks. I would recommend this approach as an initial way to start gaining knowledge of the banking field. It can definitely help open doors after graduation.

Franchise Owners

OVERVIEW

A *franchise owner* contracts with a company to sell that company's products or services. After paying an initial fee and agreeing to pay the company a certain percentage of revenue, the franchise owner can use the company's name, logo, and guidance. McDonald's, Subway, and KFC are some of the top franchised companies that have locations all across the country. Franchises, however, are not limited to the fast food industry. Today, franchises are available in a wide variety of business areas including computer service, lawn care, real estate, and even hair salons. According to a survey by PricewaterhouseCoopers, the franchising sector creates 18 million jobs in the United States and yields $1.53 trillion in economic output annually.

HISTORY

Know anybody with an antique Singer sewing machine? Chances are, it was originally sold by one of the first franchise operations. During the Civil War, the Singer Sewing Machine Company recognized the cost-efficiency of franchising and allowed dealers across the country to sell its sewing machines. Coca-Cola, as well as the Ford Motor Company and other automobile manufacturers, followed Singer's lead in the early 20th century by granting individuals the rights to sell their products. Franchising, however, didn't fully catch on until after World War II, when the needs for products and services across the country boomed, right along with the population. Ray Kroc jumped on the bandwagon with his McDonald's restaurants in the 1950s. Since then, the McDonald's

QUICK FACTS

School Subjects
Business
Mathematics

Personal Skills
Following instructions
Leadership/management

Work Environment
Primarily indoors
Primarily one location

Minimum Education Level
Some postsecondary training

Salary Range
$0 to $30,000 to $100,000+

Certification or Licensing
Required by certain
  franchisers (certification)
Required by certain states
  (licensing)

Outlook
About as fast as the average

DOT
N/A

GOE
N/A

NOC
N/A

O*NET-SOC
N/A

franchise has become one of the top money-making franchise opportunities of all time.

Franchises have changed somewhat over the last 20 to 30 years. Abuses of the franchise system brought new government regulations in the 1970s, and the government has been actively involved in protecting the rights of both franchisers and franchisees. Also, single-unit ownership, the "mom and pop" operations, is giving way to multiple-unit ownership; a majority of franchisees now own more than one of the franchiser's units.

THE JOB

Today, industry experts report that franchises are responsible for nearly 50 percent of all retail sales in the United States, and this figure is expected to grow through the 21st century. *Franchisers* (those companies that sell franchise businesses) and *franchisees* (those who buy the businesses) are sharing in the more than $1.5 trillion a year that franchise businesses take in. While everyone probably has a favorite business or two—maybe the neighborhood Krispy Kreme with its fresh crullers or the 7-Eleven down the street with its gallon-sized sodas—not everyone may realize that these are franchised establishments. For those interested in starting their own businesses, becoming franchisees may offer just the right mix of risk and security. Any new business venture comes with a certain amount of risk, but franchises offer the new owners the security of a name and product that customers are used to and are willing to seek out. Someone with money to invest, the willingness to work hard and sometimes long hours, and the desire to operate a retail business may be able to become a successful franchisee, sharing in the franchiser's success.

There's a franchise for practically every type of product and service imaginable. In addition to the familiar McDonald's and Burger King, other franchise operations exist: businesses that offer temporary employment services, maid services, weight control centers, and custom picture framing, to name a few. The International Franchise Association (IFA), in fact, reports that there are approximately 75 different industries that make use of the franchise system. No matter what business a person is interested in, there are probably franchise opportunities available.

Depending on the size and nature of the franchise, owners' responsibilities will differ. Those who are able to make a large initial investment may also be able to hire managers and staff members to assist them. Those running a smaller business will need to handle most, if not all, of the job responsibilities themselves. Though there should be assistance from the franchiser in terms of training, marketing guidance, and established business systems, the business is essentially the franchisee's own. The franchisee has paid an initial franchise fee, makes royalty payments to the franchiser, purchased equipment, and rented business space. Any franchisee must handle administrative details, such as record-keeping, creating budgets, and preparing reports for the franchiser. A franchisee is also responsible for hiring (and firing) employees, scheduling work hours, preparing payroll, and keeping track of inventory. Using the franchiser's marketing methods, the franchisee advertises the business. The practices and systems of franchisers differ, so those interested in this work need to carefully research the franchise before buying into it.

Some owners work directly with the clientele. Of course, someone who owns multiple units of the McDonald's franchise probably won't be taking orders at the counter; but someone who owns a single unit of a smaller operation, like a pool maintenance service, may be actively involved in the work at hand, in dealing with the customers, and in finding new customers.

Donna Weber of Redmond, Washington, owns a Jazzercise franchise. Jazzercise is the world's largest dance fitness franchise corporation, with 6,800 instructors leading more than 30,000 classes weekly in 30 countries. "I own and teach seven Jazzercise classes a week in two suburbs around the Seattle area," Weber says. After investing with an initial low franchise fee, Weber went through considerable training and testing; the training involves instruction on exercise physiology, dance/exercise technique, and safety issues, as well as instruction on the business aspect of owning a franchise. After training, Weber received certification and started her business. She pays a monthly fee to Jazzercise and in return receives choreography notes to new songs and videos demonstrating the exercises.

In addition to conducting classes, Weber spends some part of every workday preparing paperwork for the corporate headquarters. "I keep track of my students' attendance and write personal postcards to those I haven't seen in a while, those who are having birthdays, those who need some personal recognition for a job well done, etc.," says Weber, who must also regularly learn new routines. "I teach three different formats," she says, "regular aerobics, step, and a circuit-training class each week, so there is a lot of prep to do a good, safe class."

The franchisee's experience will be affected by the name recognition of the business. If it's a fairly new business, the franchisee may have to take on much of the responsibility of promoting it. If it is a

An owner of a Quizno's sandwich shop franchise prepares to check in an order of fresh bread that has just been delivered. *(David Zalubowski, AP Photo)*

well-established business, customers and clients already know what to expect from the operation.

REQUIREMENTS

High School

Business, math, economics, and accounting courses will be the most valuable to you in preparing for franchise ownership. Before buying into a franchise, you'll have to do a lot of research into the company, analyzing local demographics to determine whether a business is a sound investment. English classes will help you develop the research skills you'll need. In addition, you will need to hone your communication skills, which will be essential in establishing relationships with franchisers and customers. Take computer classes since it is virtually impossible to work in today's business world without knowing how to use a computer or the Web. If you already know of a particular area that interests you—such as food service, fashion, or, like Donna Weber, fitness—take classes that will help you learn more about it. Such classes may include home economics, art, dance, or physical education.

Postsecondary Training

Because there is such a variety of franchise opportunities available, there is no single educational path for everyone to take on the road to owning a franchise. Keep in mind, however, that when franchisers review your application for the right to purchase a unit, they'll take into consideration your previous experience in the area. Obviously, a real estate company is unlikely to take a risk on you if you've never had any experience as a broker. In addition, there are some franchise opportunities that require degrees; for example, to own an environmental consulting agency, a business that helps companies meet government environmental standards, you'll have to be an engineer or geologist (careers that, in most cases, require at least a bachelor's degree). But there are also many companies willing to sell to someone wanting to break into a new business. Franchisers will often include special training as part of the initial franchise fee.

Experts in the field stress the importance of gaining work experience before starting out with your own business. Hone your sales, management, and people skills and take the time to learn about the industry that interests you. Even if you don't plan on getting a college degree, consider taking some college-level courses in subjects such as business and finance. One recent survey of franchisees found that over 80 percent had attended college or had a college degree. This reflects the fact that many franchisees have worked for many years in other professions in order to have the money and security needed for starting new businesses. Some organizations and schools, for example, the Schulze School of Entrepreneurship at the University of St. Thomas (http://www.stthomas.edu/cob/schoolofentrepreneurship/default.html), offer courses for prospective franchisees.

Certification or Licensing

Some franchisers have their own certification process and require their franchisees to go through training. You may also want to receive the certification certified franchise executive offered by the Institute for Certified Franchise Executives, an organization affiliated with the IFA. This certification involves completing a certain number of courses in topics such as economics and franchise law, participating in events such as seminars or conventions, and work experience. Although certification is voluntary, it will show your level of education and commitment to the field as well as give you the opportunity to network with other franchise professionals.

You may also need to obtain a small business license to own a franchise unit in your state. Regulations vary depending on the state and the type of business, so it is important that you check with your state's licensing board for specifics before you invest in a franchise.

Other Requirements

As with any small business, you need self-motivation and discipline in order to make your franchise unit successful. Though you'll have some help from your franchiser, the responsibilities of ownership are your own. You'll also need a good credit rating to be eligible for a bank loan, or you'll need enough money of your own for the initial investment. You should be fairly cautious—many people are taken every year in fraudulent franchise schemes—but at the same time feel comfortable taking some risks.

EXPLORING

One relatively easy way to learn about franchising is to do some research on the Web. The International Franchise Association, for example, hosts a very informative Web site (http://www.franchise.org). The association also offers the magazine *Franchising World*. Also, check out your public library or bookstores for the many business magazines that report on small business opportunities. Many of these magazines, such as *Entrepreneur* (http://www.entrepreneur.com), publish special editions dealing specifically with franchises.

Join your high school's business club, a group that may give you the opportunity to meet business leaders in your community. Find a local franchise owner and ask to meet with him or her for an information interview. Discuss the pros and cons of franchise

The Top 10 Fastest Growing Franchises, 2008

1. Jan-Pro Franchising International (commercial cleaning)
2. 7-Eleven Inc. (convenience store)
3. Subway (fast food)
4. Jani-King (commercial cleaning service)
5. Dunkin' Donuts
6. Jackson Hewitt Tax Service
7. Bonus Building Care (commercial cleaning)
8. Instant Tax Service
9. Liberty Tax Service
10. RE/MAX International Inc. (real estate)

Source: *Entrepreneur* (http://www.entrepreneur.com)

ownership, find out about the owner's educational and professional background, and ask them for general advice. In addition, most franchise companies will send you brochures about their franchise opportunities. Request some information and read about what's involved in owning a franchise unit.

Think about what industry interests you, such as services, fast food, health and fitness, or computers. Come up with your own ideas for a franchise business and do some research to find out if this business already exists. If it does, there may be a part-time or summer job opportunity there for you. If it doesn't, keep the idea in mind for your future but go ahead and get some work experience now. Many franchises hire high school students, and even if you end up working at a Subway when what you're really interested in is lawn care, you'll still be gaining valuable experience dealing with customers, handling sales, and working with others.

EMPLOYERS

There are a number of franchise directories available that list hundreds of franchise opportunities in diverse areas. While some franchisers sell units all across the country, others only do business in a few states. Some of the most successful franchises can guarantee a franchisee great revenue, but these franchise units can require hundreds of thousands of dollars in initial investment.

Many franchisees own more than one franchise unit with a company; some even tie two different franchises together in a practice called "cross-branding." For example, a franchisee may own a pizza franchise, as well as an ice cream franchise housed in the same restaurant. Another combination owners find popular is having a convenience store that also houses a fast food outlet.

STARTING OUT

Before you invest a cent, or sign any papers, you should do extensive research into the franchise, particularly if it's a fairly new company. There are many disreputable franchise operations, so you need to be certain of what you're investing in. Lawyers and franchise consultants offer their services to assist people in choosing franchises; some consultants also conduct seminars. The Federal Trade Commission publishes *A Consumer Guide to Buying a Franchise* and other relevant publications. The IFA also provides free franchise-buying advice.

You'll need money for the initial franchise fee and for the expenses of the first few years of business. You may pursue a loan from a bank, from business associates, or you may use your own savings. In some cases your start-up costs will be very low; in others you'll need money for a computer, rental of work space, equipment, signs, and staff. According to the IFA, total start-up costs can range from $20,000 or less to over $1,000,000, depending on the franchise selected and whether it is necessary to own or lease real estate to operate the business. Moreover, the initial franchise fee for most franchisers is between $20,000 and $28,000.

Some franchises can cost much less. Donna Weber's Jazzercise franchise required an initial $600 franchise fee. Though her business has been successful, she must share her gross income. "Twenty percent of that goes back to Jazzercise each month as a fee, I pay about 23 percent of the gross for monthly rent, and 8.6 percent to the state of Washington for sales tax collected on the price of my tickets. There are lots of women grossing $75,000 a year doing this, and there are some who choose to do this for fun and make nothing in return. It's all in how you make it work for you."

ADVANCEMENT

A new franchise unit usually takes a few years to turn profitable. Once the business has proven a success, franchisees may choose to invest in other franchise units with the same company. Franchise owners may also be able to afford to hire management and other staff to take on some of the many responsibilities of the business.

EARNINGS

The earnings for franchisees vary greatly depending on such factors as the type of franchise they own, the amount of money a franchisee was able to initially invest without taking a loan, the franchise's location, and the number of franchise units the franchisee owns. An International Franchise Association survey of 1,000 franchise owners found that the average yearly salary of this group was $91,630. Approximately 24 percent made more than $100,000 annually.

Since franchisees run their own businesses, they generally do not have paid sick days or holidays. In addition, they are typically responsible for providing their own insurance and retirement plans.

WORK ENVIRONMENT

Owning a franchise unit can be demanding, requiring work of 60 to 70 hours a week, but owners have the satisfaction of knowing that their business's success is a result of their own hard work. Some people look for franchise opportunities that are less demanding and may only require a part-time commitment. "I'm not getting rich," Donna Weber says, "but I love my job, and I love being my own boss. I can schedule my vacations when I want; we usually don't close our classes down, so we hire certified Jazzercise substitutes."

Franchise owners who handle all the business details personally may consider this work to be very stressful. In addition, dealing with the hiring, management, and sometimes firing of staff can also be difficult. In some situations, much of a franchisee's work will be limited to an office setting; in other situations, such as with a home inspection service or a maid service, the franchisee drives to remote sites to work with clients. Some franchises are mobile in nature, and these will involve a lot of traveling within a designated region.

OUTLOOK

While some experts say that the success rate of franchises is very high and a great deal of money can be made with a franchise unit, others say franchising isn't as successful as starting an independent business. According to the U.S. Department of Commerce, less than 5 percent of franchised outlets have failed each year since 1971. However, when reporting figures, franchisers don't always consider a unit as failing if it is under different ownership, but still in operation. The employment outlook will depend on factors such as the economy—a downturn in the economy is always most difficult for new businesses—as well as the type of franchise. Overall, though, growth should be steady and about as fast as the average.

FOR MORE INFORMATION

For information about buying a franchise and a list of AAFD-accredited franchisers, contact
American Association of Franchisees & Dealers (AAFD)
PO Box 81887
San Diego, CA 92138-1887
Tel: 800-733-9858
Email: Benefits@aafd.org
http://www.aafd.org

Visit the FTC's Web site for information on franchising, including the publication A Consumer Guide to Buying a Franchise.
Federal Trade Commission (FTC)
600 Pennsylvania Avenue, NW
Washington, DC 20580-0001

Tel: 202-326-2222
http://www.ftc.gov

For more information on franchising as well as a free newsletter, contact
FranchiseHelp
101 Executive Boulevard, 2nd Floor
Elmsford, NY 10523-1302
Tel: 800-401-1446
Email: company@franchisehelp.com
http://www.franchisehelp.com

For general information about franchising, specific franchise opportunities, and publications, contact the IFA
International Franchise Association (IFA)
1501 K Street, NW, Suite 350
Washington, DC 20005-1401
Tel: 202-628-8000
Email: ifa@franchise.org
http://www.franchise.org

Health Care Managers

OVERVIEW

Health care managers, also known as *health services managers* and *health services administrators,* direct the operation of hospitals, nursing homes, and other health care organizations. They are responsible for facilities, services, programs, staff, budgets, and relations with other organizations. There are approximately 262,000 health care managers employed in the United States.

HISTORY

Health care institutions have changed considerably since the Pennsylvania Hospital was established in Philadelphia in the mid-1700s by Benjamin Franklin and Dr. Thomas Bond. The rapid advancement of medical science, the high degree of specialization by physicians, the increasing need for technical assistants, and the need for expensive and elaborate equipment all depend on effective organization to assure efficient use. This ever-increasing complexity has brought about the growing professional occupation of hospital and health services managers.

In the past, physicians, nurses, or workers in other fields were appointed to the position of hospital administrator with little or no special training. The earliest recognition of hospital administration as a separate profession came in the 1890s when the Association of Hospital Superintendents was organized. This group, whose membership includes nearly all of the hospitals in the United States, is today known as the American Hospital Association. In the 1930s, the American College of Hospital Administrators (now the

QUICK FACTS

School Subjects
Business
English

Personal Skills
Helping/teaching
Leadership/management

Work Environment
Primarily indoors
One location with some
travel

Minimum Education Level
Bachelor's degree

Salary Range
$45,050 to $73,340 to
$127,830+

Certification or Licensing
Voluntary (certification)
Required for certain
positions (licensing)

Outlook
Faster than the average

DOT
187

GOE
14.01.01

NOC
0014

O*NET-SOC
11-9111.00

American College of Healthcare Executives) was founded to increase the standards of practice and education in the field.

The broad range of today's health care institutions includes general hospitals, medical group practices, extended care facilities, nursing homes, rehabilitation institutions, psychiatric hospitals, health maintenance organizations (HMOs), and outpatient clinics. The field of long-term care is one of the fastest growing parts of the industry; today, there are more than 15,000 nursing homes throughout the United States. Approximately 262,000 jobs, about 37 percent of them in hospitals, are held by health care managers.

THE JOB

Health care managers of hospitals and health care facilities organize and manage personnel, equipment, and auxiliary services. They hire and supervise personnel, handle budgets and fee schedules charged to patients, and establish billing procedures. In addition, they help plan space needs, purchase supplies and equipment, oversee building and equipment maintenance, and provide for mail, phones, laundry, and other services for patients and staff. In some health care institutions, many of these duties are delegated to assistants or to various department heads. These assistants may supervise operations in such clinical areas as surgery, nursing, dietary, or therapy and in such administrative areas as purchasing, finance, housekeeping, and maintenance.

The health services administrator works closely with the institution's governing board to develop plans and policies. Following the board's directions, the administrator may carry out large projects that expand and develop hospital services. Such projects include organizing fund-raising campaigns and planning new research projects.

Health services managers meet regularly with their staffs to discuss departmental goals and to address problems. Managers may organize training programs for nurses, interns, and others in cooperation with the medical staff and department heads. Health care executives also represent the health care facility at community or professional meetings.

REQUIREMENTS

High School

If you are interested in a career in health management, you should start preparing in high school by taking college preparatory classes. Because communication skills are important, take as many speech and writing classes as possible. Courses in health, business, mathematics, and computer science are also excellent choices to help you prepare for this career.

Postsecondary Training

The training required to qualify for this work depends, to a large extent, on the qualifications established by the individual employer or a facility's governing board. Most prefer people with a graduate degree in health services administration, long-term care administration, public administration, health sciences, public health, or business administration. A few require that their chief executives be physicians, while others look for people with formal training in law or general business administration as well as experience in the health care field. The future health care administrator may have a liberal arts foundation with a strong background in the social sciences or business economics.

Specialized training in health services administration is offered at both graduate and undergraduate levels. The graduate program generally takes two years to complete. Graduate students split their time between studying in the classroom and working as an administrative resident in a program-approved health care facility. Successful completion of the course work, the residency, and perhaps a thesis is required to earn the master's degree. An optional third-year fellowship provides additional work experience supervised by a mentor. During this period, the individual may work in various hospital departments as an assistant to department heads.

Certification or Licensing

The American College of Health Care Administrators (ACHCA) offers voluntary certification to nursing home and assisted living administrators who meet educational and work experience requirements and pass an examination. Certification must be renewed every five years. Contact the ACHCA for more information.

Additionally, the American College of Healthcare Executives (ACHE) offers the certified healthcare executive designation to candidates who pass an examination and meet other requirements. Fellow status is available to certified healthcare executives with advanced experience and skills. Contact the ACHE for more information.

Licensure is not a requirement for health care services executives employed in hospitals. However, all states require nursing home administrators to be licensed. Most states use the licensing exam prepared by the National Association of Boards of Examiners of Long Term Care Administrators. Because requirements vary from state to state, those considering careers in nursing home administration should contact their state's licensing body for specific licensure requirements. Furthermore, it should be noted that continuing education is now a condition of licensure in most states.

Other Requirements
Much of the work of health services managers consists of dealing with people—the hospital's governing board, the medical staff, the department heads and other employees, the patients and their families, and community leaders and businesses. Therefore, health care managers must be tactful and sympathetic.

In addition, administrators must be able to coordinate the health care facility's many related functions. They need to understand, for instance, financial operations, purchasing, organizational development, and public relations. They must also have the ability to make some decisions with speed and others with considerable study. And, of course, health services executives should have a deep interest in the care of sick and injured patients.

Special hospitals, such as mental hospitals, often employ administrators who are physicians in the facility's specialty.

EXPLORING

If you are considering a career as a health services manager, you should take advantage of opportunities in high school to develop some of the skills required in this line of work. Because administrators and other health care executives need strong leadership and communication skills, participation in clubs as a leader or active member and in debate and speech clubs is helpful. Working in your school's health center is also useful. Hospitals, nursing homes, and other health service facilities offer part-time work after school, on weekends, and during the summer. Health services executives are often willing to speak to interested students, but be sure to make an appointment first.

EMPLOYERS

Approximately 262,000 health care managers are employed in hospitals, HMOs, group medical practices, and centers for urgent care, cardiac rehabilitation, and diagnostic imaging. Opportunities are also plentiful in long-term care facilities, such as nursing homes, home health care agencies, adult day care programs, life care communities, and other residential facilities.

STARTING OUT

A student in training as an administrative resident or postgraduate fellow may be offered a job as an administrative assistant or department head by the hospital or health care facility where the residency is served. The hospital's administrator at the place of training also may assist the student in locating a job.

Job openings can also be found by contacting the university's career services office or through bulletins of state and national associations. Large professional society meetings may offer on-site notices of job openings. Positions in federal- and state-operated health care institutions are filled by the civil service or by political appointment. Appointments to armed forces hospitals are handled by the various branches of the services.

Although the majority of students prepare for this career with a four-year college program followed by graduate study, it is still possible to secure a health administration position through experience and training in subordinate jobs and working up the administrative ladder.

ADVANCEMENT

It is unusual to finish college and step into a position as an upper-level health services executive. Most new graduates first gain experience in a more specialized clinical or administrative area of a health care facility. There they can become accustomed to working with health care personnel, patients, information systems, budgets, and finances. This experience and/or graduate work often leads to promotion to department head. Those with graduate training can expect to achieve higher-level positions. Assistant administrator or vice president is often the next step and may lead to appointment as the hospital's chief executive.

EARNINGS

Salaries of health services executives depend on the type of facility, geographic location, the size of the administrative staff, the budget, and the policy of the governing board. The U.S. Department of Labor reports that the median annual earnings of medical and health services managers were $73,340 in 2006. Salaries ranged from less than $45,050 to more than $127,830. The U.S. Department of Labor reports that the mean salary of health care managers who worked in hospitals was $84,930 in 2006, and those who worked in nursing care facilities earned $71,480.

A *Modern Healthcare* survey reports the following median annual salaries for department managers in 2005: respiratory therapy, $74,700; home health care, $82,000; physical therapy, $83,700; medical imaging/diagnostic radiology, $96,000; medical records, $97,000; rehabilitation services $92,500; and nursing services, $103,400.

Some administrators receive free meals, housing, and laundry service, depending on the facility in which they are employed. They usually receive paid vacations and holidays, sick leave, hospitalization and insurance benefits, and pension programs. The executive benefits package nowadays often includes management incentive bonuses based on job performance ranging from $25,000 to $225,000.

WORK ENVIRONMENT

To perform efficiently as an executive, health services administrators usually work out of a large office. They must maintain good communication with the staff and members of various departments.

Most administrators work five and a half days a week, averaging about 55 to 60 hours. However, hours can be irregular because hospitals and other health care facilities operate around the clock; emergencies may require the manager's supervision any time of the day or night.

OUTLOOK

Because every hospital and numerous other health care facilities employ administrators, employment opportunities in health care will be good through 2016 as the industry continues to diversify and deal with the problems of financing health care for everyone. The U.S. Department of Labor predicts that employment will grow faster than the average for all occupations.

Not all areas will grow at the same rate, however. Changes in the health care system are taking place because of the need to control escalating costs. This will have the greatest impact on hospitals, traditionally the largest employer of health services executives. The number of hospitals is declining as separate companies are set up to provide services such as ambulatory surgery, alcohol and drug rehabilitation, or home health care. So, while hospitals may offer fewer jobs, many new openings are expected to be available in other health care settings. Employment will grow the fastest in home health care services and in the offices and clinics of medical practitioners. There will also be more opportunities with health care management companies that provide management services to hospitals and other organizations, as well as with specific departments such as emergency, managed care contract negotiations, information management systems, and physician recruiting.

Many colleges and universities are reporting more graduates in health services administration than hospitals and other health care facilities can employ. As a result, competition for administrative jobs will be stiff. However, many starting executives can find jobs working in health care settings other than hospitals, or they may be offered jobs at the department head or staff levels.

With hospitals adopting a more business-like approach aimed at lowering costs and increasing earnings, demand for M.B.A. graduates should remain steady. Individuals who have strong people skills and business or management knowledge will find excellent opportunities as administrators in nursing homes and other long-term facilities.

FOR MORE INFORMATION

For information on state licensing, certification, and student resources, contact

American College of Health Care Administrators
12100 Sunset Hills Road, Suite 130
Reston, VA 20190-3233
Tel: 703-739-7900
Email: certification@achca.org
http://www.achca.org

For general information on health care management, contact
American College of Healthcare Executives
One North Franklin Street, Suite 1700
Chicago, IL 60606-3529
Tel: 312-424-2800
Email: geninfo@ache.org
http://www.ache.org

For information on health care administration careers, scholarships, and accredited programs, contact
Association of University Programs in Health Administration
2000 North 14th Street, Suite 780
Arlington, VA 22201-2543
Tel: 703-894-0940
Email: aupha@aupha.org
http://www.aupha.org

For information about employment opportunities in ambulatory care management and medical group practices, contact

Medical Group Management Association
104 Inverness Terrace East
Englewood, CO 80112-5306
Tel: 877-275-6462
Email: service@mgma.com
http://www.mgma.org

For information on licensure, contact
National Association of Boards of Examiners of Long Term
  Care Administrators
1444 I Street, NW, Suite 700
Washington, DC 20005-6542
Tel: 202-712-9040
Email: nab@bostrom.com
http://www.nabweb.org

*For publications, news releases, and information from recent health
care conferences, contact*
National Health Council
1730 M Street, NW, Suite 500
Washington, DC 20036-4561
Tel: 202-785-3910
Email: info@nhcouncil.org
http://www.nationalhealthcouncil.org

*For information about careers in health care office management,
contact*
Professional Association of Health Care Office Management
4700 West Lake Avenue
Glenview, IL 60025-1468
Tel: 800-451-9311
http://www.pahcom.com

*For comprehensive information about the career of health care
manager, visit*
Make a Difference: Discover a Career in Healthcare Management!
http://www.healthmanagementcareers.org

INTERVIEW

*Dr. Mary K. Madsen is a professor and the director of the Health
Care Administration & Informatics Program at the University of
Wisconsin-Milwaukee (UWM). She discussed her career and the*

education of health care administration students with the editors of Careers in Focus: Business Managers.

Q. Can you tell us about your program and your background?
A. We offer a B.S. in health care administration (HCA) with a minor in business administration. We are a fully certified member of the Association of University Programs in Health Administration. There are approximately 200 undergraduate programs in HCA in the United States and only 35 are fully certified programs. The program of study consists of 128 credits including the minor. We also have a master's program in health care informatics.

My background consists of two degrees in nursing (B.S., M.S.N.), and my Ph.D. is in child and family studies. For 10 years, I was the director of an interdisciplinary rehabilitation clinic for individuals with neurogenic impairments (e.g., stroke, multiple sclerosis, head injury) at UWM. I have been teaching at UWM since 1973.

Q. Can you tell us about the internship opportunities that are available to students in your program?
A. Students are required to take at least one internship before graduation. They may take as many as three internships. Their internships are primarily in the Milwaukee area or in Waukesha [a suburb of Milwaukee]. Two students have done internships through the University of Rochester in England. The experiences are varied (e.g., hospitals, nursing homes, medical sales, outpatient clinics, health clubs, etc.). We have added a Desire2Learn capstone course, which consists of quizzes from required readings, discussion threads, and a case study. The internship is 128 hours during the course of one semester. We gather mid-semester and finalize evaluations of the students and students' assessment of the agencies in which they are interning.

Q. What is one thing that young people may not know about a career in health care management?
A. Most students feel that they can just walk into an entry-level health care position and do their job. They are not aware of the complex political and people-person skills that they need. They see this to some extent in their internships, but are probably still a little naïve about it when they take their first job.

Q. What types of students pursue study in your program?

A. Approximately 60 percent of the students are business oriented as deemed from their temperament sorter. They take the Myers-Briggs Temperament Sorter in their sophomore year. The students basically like to make decisions.

Q. What advice would you offer health care administration majors as they graduate and look for jobs?

A. The advice that I would give to our graduates is that at some point they should get a graduate degree. Most students are uncertain whether they should go directly to a master's program or work first. I believe that most of our students get an additional degree. We have a couple students who have gone back for a nursing degree upon completion of their HCA degree.

Hotel and Motel Managers

OVERVIEW

Hotel and motel managers, sometimes called *lodging managers*, are ultimately responsible for the business of running their hotel or motel smoothly and efficiently. Larger establishments may have several managers accountable for different departments. In turn, these departmental managers report to the *general manager*. The general manager's many duties include managing personnel, financial operations, and promotional activities. Lodging managers hold approximately 71,000 jobs in the United States.

HISTORY

As travel became more frequent in the United States and around the world, the idea of a comfortable place for travelers to stay and rest became a reality. The earliest lodging places were probably simple shelters with no food or running water available. Better roads and means of transportation allowed more people the luxury of travel, which in turn raised the standard of lodging. The early inns, called *mansiones*, were often located along roads. They offered a bed and, sometimes, a meal. The first hotel and motel managers were the owners themselves. They were responsible for maintaining the rooms, collecting payment, and providing food and drink to guests.

As hotels and motels began to consolidate, and chains were built, managers became more important. Many times, a single person, or family, would own numerous hotel or motel properties, and hire reliable people to help manage the business. Managers were trusted

QUICK FACTS

School Subjects
Business
Mathematics
Speech

Personal Skills
Helping/teaching
Leadership/management

Work Environment
Primarily indoors
Primarily one location

Minimum Education Level
Associate's degree

Salary Range
$25,120 to $42,320 to $82,510+

Certification or Licensing
Voluntary

Outlook
About as fast as the average

DOT
187

GOE
11.01.01

NOC
0632

O*NET-SOC
11-9081.00

to run the establishments properly, turn a profit, and make sure rooms were filled.

THE JOB

Hotel and motel managers are responsible for the overall supervision of their establishment, the different departments, and their staff. They follow operating guidelines set by the owners, or if part of a chain, by the main headquarters and executive board. A general manager, often abbreviated to GM, allocates funds to all departments, approves expenditures, sets room rates, and establishes standards for food and beverage service, decor, and all guest services. GMs tour their property every day, usually with the head of the housekeeping department, to make certain everything is clean and orderly. GMs are responsible for keeping their establishment's accounting books in order, doing or approving the advertising and marketing, maintaining and ordering supplies, and interviewing and training new employees. However, in large hotels and motels, the GM is usually supported by one or more assistants and departmental managers.

Some hotels and motels still employ *resident managers,* who live on the premises and are on call 24 hours a day, in case of emergencies. Resident managers work regular eight-hour shifts daily, attending to the duties of the hotel or motel. In many modern establishments, the general manager has replaced the resident manager.

In large hotels and motels, departmental managers include the following:

Front office managers supervise the activity and staff of the front desk. They direct reservations and sleeping room assignments. Front office managers make sure that all guests are treated courteously and check-in and check-out periods are managed smoothly. Any guest complaints or problems are usually directed to the front desk first—front office managers are responsible for rectifying all customer complaints before they reach the general manager.

Executive housekeepers are managers who supervise the work of the room attendants, housekeepers, janitors, gardeners, and the laundry staff. Depending on the size and structure of the hotel, they may also be in charge of ordering cleaning supplies, linens, towels, and toiletries. Some executive housekeepers may be responsible for dealing with suppliers and vendors.

Personnel managers head human resources or personnel departments. They hire and fire employees and work with other personnel employees such as training managers, benefits coordinators, and employee relations managers.

Training managers oversee the hotel's management training program. Other employees in this department include *benefits coordinators,* who handle employee benefits such as health insurance and pension plans, and *employee relations managers,* who deal with employee rights and grievances with an overall goal of creating a positive and productive work atmosphere.

A *security manager,* sometimes known as a *director of hotel security,* is entrusted with the protection of the guests, workers, and grounds and property of the hotel.

Food and beverage managers are responsible for all food service operations in the hotel—from restaurants, cocktail lounges and banquets to room service. They supervise food and service quality and preparation, order supplies from different vendors, and estimate food costs.

Restaurant managers oversee the daily operation of hotel or motel restaurants. They manage employees such as waiters, buspersons, hosts, bartenders, and cooks and bakers. They also resolve customer complaints. They are responsible for all food service operations in the hotel or motel—from restaurants, cocktail lounges, and banquets to room service. They supervise food and service quality and preparation, order supplies from different vendors, and estimate food costs.

Large hotels and motels can profit by marketing their facilities for conventions, meetings, and special events. *Convention services managers* are in charge of coordinating such activities. The convention

Did You Know?

- There were fewer than 10,000 hotels in 1900. In 2006, there were 62,000 hotel properties in the United States.
- Approximately 75 percent of hotels employ fewer than 20 workers.
- The average rate for a hotel room was $97.78 in 2006.
- Approximately one in eight Americans are employed either directly or indirectly in the hospitality and travel industries.
- Forty-four percent of lodging customers are transient business travelers and 56 percent are on vacation or traveling for family or other personal reasons.
- Employment of lodging managers is expected to grow by 12 percent from 2006 to 2016.

Source: American Hotel and Lodging Association, U.S. Department of Labor

Hotel managers must have excellent communication skills in order to successfully interact with customers. (*Jeff Greenberg, The Image Works*)

services manager takes care of all necessary details, such as blocking sleeping rooms for the group, arranging for meeting rooms or ballrooms, and resolving any problems that arise.

Hotel chains employ specialized managers to ensure that its hotels are being operated appropriately and in a financially sound manner. *Regional operations managers* travel throughout a specific geographic region to see that hotel chain members are operated and maintained according to the guidelines and standards set by the company. *Branch operations managers* reorganize hotels that are doing poorly financially, or set up a new hotel operation.

REQUIREMENTS

High School

It's a good idea to begin preparing for a career in hotel management while in high school. Concentrate on a business-oriented curriculum, with classes in finance, accounting, and mathematics. Since computers are widely used in the hotel setting for reservations, accounting, and management of supplies, it is important that you become computer literate. Brush up on your communication skills while in high school. You'll need them when giving direction and supervision to a large and diverse staff. Take English classes and other courses, such as speech or drama, that will give you the chance to polish your grammar and speaking skills. A second language, especially Spanish, French, or Japanese, will be very helpful to you in the future.

Postsecondary Training

While you should be able to get a starting position at a hotel or motel with only a high school diploma, many companies now require management trainees to have a minimum of a bachelor's degree in hotel and restaurant management. Numerous community and junior colleges and some universities offer associate's, bachelor's, or graduate degree programs in hotel or restaurant management. In addition, technical, vocational, and trade schools and other institutions offer hotel business programs resulting in a formal recognition of training, such as a certificate.

Classes in hotel management cover topics such as administration, marketing, housekeeping, hotel maintenance, and computer skills. To complement class instruction, most programs require students to work on site at a hotel.

Many hotels and motels will also consider candidates with liberal arts degrees or degrees in such fields as business management and public relations if they are highly qualified and talented.

Visit the American Hotel and Lodging Association's Web site, http://www.ahla.com/products_list_schools.asp, for a list of colleges and universities that offer degrees in hospitality and hotel management.

Certification or Licensing

Certification for this job is not a requirement, though it is recognized by many as a measurement of industry knowledge and job experience. The Educational Institute of the American Hotel and Lodging Association offers a variety of certifications for hotel and motel managers, including certified hotel administrator, certified lodging manager, certified lodging security director, certified food and beverage executive, certified hospitality housekeeping executive, certified human resources executive, certified engineering operations executive, certified hospitality revenue manager, and certified lodging security supervisor. Contact the institute for more information on these certifications.

High school juniors and seniors who are interested in working in the hospitality industry can take advantage of the Educational Institute of the American Hotel and Lodging Association's Lodging Management Program. The program combines classroom learning with work experience in the hospitality industry. Graduating seniors who pass examinations and work in the lodging industry for at least 30 days receive the certified rooms division specialist designation. Visit http://www.lodgingmanagement.org for more information.

Other Requirements

Managers are strong leaders who have a flair for organization and communication and, most important, work well with all types of people. To keep the hotel or motel running smoothly, general managers need to establish policies and procedures and make certain their directions are followed. Managing can sometimes be stressful, and managers need to keep a cool demeanor when dealing with difficult situations that come their way.

Vlato Lemick, general manager and owner of several hotels in the Chicago area, considers dealing with customer complaints to be one of his most challenging job duties. "Problems do reach my desk, and I have to take care of them." Does he only give attention to the important problems? "No," he says firmly. "No complaint or request should be considered unimportant."

EXPLORING

You can test your interest in this career firsthand by visiting a local hotel or motel and spending a day at the front desk, or better yet, with the general manager. Most high schools have a job shadowing program that introduces students to various careers. If your school doesn't have such a program, talk with your counseling center about implementing one.

Working in hospitality is really the best way to explore the field. Part-time jobs in any department, no matter how small, will give you important business experience. Here's a success story to inspire you. Keith Pierce's first hotel job was loading dishwashers at the Waldorf Astoria. Many dishes later, armed with a college degree and work experience, Pierce was promoted to vice president of Wingate Hotels.

EMPLOYERS

There are approximately 71,000 hotel and motel managers working in the United States. Fifty-four percent of these workers own their own hotel or motel.

Some major employers in the industry are Wyndham Worldwide (Days Inn, Super 8, Ramada, Howard Johnson, and Travelodge), Inter-Continental Hotels Group (Holiday Inn), Hilton Hotels Corporation (Doubletree, Embassy Suites, Hampton Inn, and Hilton), Starwood Hotels and Resorts (Sheraton, Westin, W Hotels, and Le Parker Meridien), and Choice Hotels International Inc. (Comfort Inn, Econo Lodge, and Sleep Inn). These companies have properties located nationwide and abroad. Marriott International Inc., another international player, offers a fast-track management program for qualified employees and has been known to encourage career advancement for minorities and women.

Long-term experience is important in this industry. It is wise to work at least one year at a company before moving to another. Employers are likely to question applicants who have had more than four employers in less than two years.

STARTING OUT

The position of general manager is one of the top rungs on this career ladder. It's unlikely this would be your first industry job. In today's highly technical age, experience, though still important, is not enough for job advancement. Most candidates have some postsecondary education; many have at least a bachelor's degree in hotel and restaurant management. Graduates entering the hotel industry usually pay their dues by working as assistant managers, assistant departmental managers, or shift managers. Many hotels and motels have specific management training programs for their management-bound employees. Employees are encouraged to work different desks so they will be knowledgeable about each department.

Your school's career center, the local library, and the Internet can all be helpful when researching college programs or specific businesses.

ADVANCEMENT

The average tenure of a general manager is between six and seven years; those who have worked as a GM for 10 years or more usually view their job as a lifetime commitment. Managers who leave the profession usually advance to the regional or even national area of hotel and motel management, such as property management or the administrative or financial departments of the lodging chain. Some may opt to open their own hotel or motel franchises or even operate a small inn or bed and breakfast. The management skills learned as a general manager can be successfully utilized in any avenue of business.

EARNINGS

Salary figures vary according to the worker's level of expertise, the lodging establishment, the duties involved, the size of the hotel or motel, and its location. General managers working in large urban areas can expect to have more responsibilities and higher compensation than those at smaller inns in rural areas.

According to the U.S. Department of Labor, lodging managers reported a median yearly income of $42,320 in 2006. The lowest paid 10 percent earned less than $25,120 annually, and the highest paid 10 percent made more than $82,510 per year. Managers may receive bonuses of 20 to 25 percent of their base salary when conditions are favorable, such as during a strong economy and when managers have increased business. These bonuses can often boost earnings by thousands of dollars.

Managers receive paid vacation and sick days and other benefits, such as medical and life insurance, and pension or profit-sharing plans. They may also receive free or discounted lodging, meals, parking, and laundry, as well as financial assistance with education.

WORK ENVIRONMENT

Don't expect to manage a 200-room hotel sitting behind a desk. General managers make at least one property walk-through a day, inspecting the condition of the hotel. The rest of the day is spent returning phone calls, meeting with clients, and running from one department to another. Managers do not have nine-to-five days; they usually work an average of 55 hours a week. Weekends and holidays are no exceptions. Off-duty managers are sometimes called back to work in cases of emergency—night or day—and they don't go home until the problem is solved. Managers interact with many different people, such as hotel or motel staff, tourists in town to see the sights, business people attending conventions, and numerous other professionals in the hospitality industry. Not everyone is polite or reasonable, and managers must be able to "think on their feet" and work calmly in difficult situations.

OUTLOOK

Overall, employment for lodging managers is predicted to grow about as fast as the average for all occupations through 2016, according to the U.S. Department of Labor. Many factors influence the employment of managers, including hotel consolidations that mean layoffs for redundant workers and the increasing number of budget hotels and motels with fewer extras, such as a restaurant or room service. Hotels and motels with fewer offerings need fewer managers.

Additionally, the travel and hospitality industry is very sensitive to economic developments. During weak economic times, people travel less often for pleasure—which means fewer tourists in need of lodging. Businesses also cut back on their expenses by limiting or eliminating business travel and using other methods, such as teleconferencing, to meet with clients who are in different locations. This also means fewer customers for hotels and motels.

World events also have a major influence on the travel and hospitality industry. For example, the terrorist attacks in the United States in 2001 dramatically reduced the number of people willing to travel for business and pleasure. A lack of customers translated into layoffs in the industry. According to the publication *National Hotel Executive,* approximately 360,000 people in the hotel sector alone lost their jobs in the three months after the attacks.

Nevertheless, industry experts predict a rebound from such slow times. Hotels and other places of lodging continue to be built (more than 600 new properties were built in the United States in 2007), and managers are needed to run them. College graduates with degrees in hotel or restaurant management, or a similar business degree, will have the best opportunities, as will managers with excellent work experience and those with certification. Other opportunities will become available as current managers move to other occupations, retire, or leave the workforce for other reasons.

FOR MORE INFORMATION

For information on careers in hotel management, contact
American Hotel and Lodging Association
1201 New York Avenue, NW, Suite 600
Washington, DC 20005-3931
Tel: 202-289-3100
Email: info@ahla.com
http://www.ahla.com

For information on internships, scholarships, and certification requirements, contact
Educational Institute of the American Hotel and Lodging Association
800 North Magnolia Avenue, Suite 300
Orlando, FL 32803-3271
Tel: 800-752-4567
Email: eiinfo@ahla.com
http://www.ei-ahla.org

For information and a listing of hostels worldwide, contact
Hostelling International USA
8401 Colesville Road, Suite 600
Silver Spring, MD 20910-6339

Tel: 301-495-1240
http://www.hiusa.org

For information on sales and marketing careers in hospitality, contact
Hospitality Sales and Marketing Association International
8201 Greensboro Drive, Suite 300
McLean, VA 22102-3814
Tel: 703-610-9024
Email: info@hsmai.org
http://www.hsmai.org

For education information and a list of available educational programs, contact
**International Council on Hotel, Restaurant and Institutional
    Education**
2810 North Parham Road, Suite 230
Richmond, VA 23294-4422
Tel: 804-346-4800
Email: info@chrie.org
http://chrie.org

For information on careers, education, and certification programs, contact
International Executive Housekeepers Association
1001 Eastwind Drive, Suite 301
Westerville, OH 43081-3361
Tel: 800-200-6342
Email: excel@ieha.org
http://www.ieha.org

INTERVIEW

David Semadeni has held a wide variety of management positions at top hotels throughout the world—including the Grand Hotel Victoria-Jungfrau, Interlaken, Switzerland; Gran Hotel Velazques, Madrid, Spain; Hotel d'Angleterre, Copenhagen, Denmark; Royal Hotel, San Remo, Italy; Suvretta House, San Moritz, Switzerland; as well as in the United States at the Sheraton-Boston Hotel, the New York Sheraton, the St. Regis-Sheraton (New York City), Sheraton Plaza (Chicago), The Ritz-Carlton (Chicago), Four Seasons (Philadelphia), Bourbon Orleans Hotel (New Orleans), and Brazilian Court (Palm Beach). He is currently the president of Amcal Management Corp, a company that manages and consults on hotels, condominiums, homeowner and trade associations, clubs, restaurants, and residential property. David discussed his career with the editors of Careers in Focus: Business Managers.

Q. Why did you decide to become a hotel manager/administrator?

A. My parents had a hotel in Scotland. I was born there, grew up in a hotel, graduated from hotel school, worked the summers at school from 16 onwards in hotels in Europe, so essentially I don't really know any better!

Q. What have been your most rewarding experiences in the hospitality field?

A. • Taking a hotel from a hole in the ground to fully operational.
• Mentoring students, employees, and associates and seeing them succeed.
• Running a number of the great hotels in the U.S. and working in others around the world.
• Starting my own company with the help of friends in the business.

Q. What advice would you give to high school students who are interested in entering the hospitality field?

A. • Learn about the industry by working in it part time after school.
• Join a magnet or career academy program at your high school, if available in your school district.
• Intern or at least go on a shadowing opportunity at a local hotel during your summer holidays.
• Express your interest in finding out about a hospitality career by contacting a local hotel general manager and asking for advice.

Q. What are the most important professional qualities for hotel managers?

A. • Attaining formal education commensurate with position. A general manager should have at least an undergraduate degree. At upper-strata hotels a master's or equivalent is required. The days of working one's way up from a bellman without some formal education are pretty well over.
• Experience level for position

- Skills: languages, extramural activities
- Integrity and persistence

Q. What is the future employment outlook in the field?

A. Excellent. And, as in any career, rewards will come to those who have the background, experience, and skills for the position to whatever level they aspire.

Hotel Executive Housekeepers

OVERVIEW

Hotel executive housekeepers direct and control the staff and operations of housekeeping departments within a hotel. They are responsible for ensuring that the rooms and property are clean and presentable. Millions of people are employed at all levels of housekeeping and in different fields, such as lodging, hospitals, nursing homes, retail, and schools. The International Executive Housekeepers Association, an organization for housekeeping executives, has more than 3,500 members.

HISTORY

A large part of any hotel's reputation rests on its appearance. A posh hotel would lose some of its grandeur if the lobby looked cluttered and dirty. Hotel patrons don't mind paying higher room fees when they are guaranteed some measure of luxury, if only for a night or two. Because all guests, whether paying $29.99 a night at the Motel 6 or $300+ a night at the Hotel Intercontinental, expect their rooms to be neat and orderly, the housekeeping staff is vital to the success of any motel or hotel. At the helm of the hotel housekeeping department is the executive housekeeper, also known as the *director of housekeeping services.*

The earliest housekeeping executives were most probably owners of the hotel. Often the innkeepers did not have any help aside from family members; they were responsible for cleaning the inn, cooking food, showing guests to their rooms, and maintaining records.

QUICK FACTS

School Subjects
Business
Mathematics

Personal Skills
Helping/teaching
Leadership/management

Work Environment
Primarily indoors
Primarily one location

Minimum Education Level
Associate's degree

Salary Range
$25,120 to $28,780 to $82,510+

Certification or Licensing
Recommended

Outlook
About as fast as the average

DOT
187

GOE
11.01.01

NOC
6213

O*NET-SOC
11-9081.00, 37-1011.00, 37-1011.01

Eventually, hotels became bigger, and in some cases they merged with other hotels to form chains and franchises. Soon, owners were forced to hire employees to help with the operations of the hotel.

This job is not defined by a mop and bucket. Executive house-keepers, one of the highest managerial positions in hospitality, are responsible for overseeing the cleanliness and appearance of the hotel. They supervise a team of cleaning professionals who keep the hotel in top condition.

Executive housekeepers need to be comfortable working with computers, a vital tool in maintaining paperwork, vendor informa-tion, and supply inventory. They also need to be familiar with new techniques to expedite the process of cleaning without sacrificing thoroughness. Robotics, for example, has helped the workload of cleaners. Much of the lifting and cleaning of heavy pieces of furni-ture is now done by machinery. Large lobby areas are now cleaned by automatic washers instead of hand mops. Cleaning solutions have been improved to do their job faster and better, yet remain friendly to different woods and fabrics as well as the environment.

THE JOB

The primary duty of executive housekeepers is to ensure the cleanli-ness of the hotel. They supervise, coordinate, and direct the activities of the hotel housekeeping department. They determine the cleaning needs of different areas in the hotel—lobby, sleeping rooms, restau-rants, pools—and schedule cleaning crews accordingly. Areas are inspected regularly to make certain safety standards and depart-mental policies are being met. They hire and train the cleaning staff, as well as recommend promotions, transfers, and, if necessary, dis-missals. Executive housekeepers are also responsible for keeping inventory of cleaning supplies and equipment, as well as hotel linens, towels, and soaps. They deal directly with vendors to learn about the latest in cleaning solutions, equipment, and techniques.

The cleaning of uniforms worn by the hotel staff, as well as all hotel laundry, is among the executive housekeepers' responsibilities. They prepare reports concerning room occupancy, department bud-get expenses, and employee work records for payroll. Some executive housekeepers may help decorate the hotel. Some also direct the setup for conventions and banquets.

Though executive housekeepers may share in some of the clean-ing duties, in larger hotels their role is mostly administrative. Some extremely busy hotels may even hire *assistant executive housekeepers* or *assistant directors* to share in the administrative duties of keeping house. *Shift supervisors* are directly responsible for the employees and the work done on their particular shift. (Hotels operate 24 hours a day, so many have implemented a three-shift system.) *Floor managers* and *inspectors* supervise the team of room attendants assigned to a particular floor. A *status person* handles any special requests a guest might make while at the hotel.

The cleaning staff also keeps the lobby neat and orderly. They empty trash cans and ashtrays, gather glasses from the lobby tables, dust furniture, clean mirrors, and vacuum carpets and rugs. Hotel restaurants are also cleaned and maintained throughout the day. Pools and health clubs must be cleaned and sanitized. *Room attendants* are responsible for the guest rooms. They tidy sleeping rooms and bathrooms, replenish towels, soaps, shampoos, and lotions as well as attend to any special requests for cribs, ironing boards, or extra supplies. They also stock and keep records of the mini-bar.

REQUIREMENTS
High School
Business, general science, and mathematics classes will give you a solid educational foundation for working in this field. Speech and English courses will boost your communication skills.

Postsecondary Training
Though hotels recognize the importance of experience, with today's competitive market, it is increasingly important to have further education. A bachelor's degree in hotel management is your best bet, but associate's degrees are valued as well. Emphasize course work in business administration, accounting, budgeting, and economics. Classes in communication, sociology, and psychology will prove helpful in dealing with a large, diverse staff. Other useful classes are interior design and purchasing.

Certification or Licensing
Certification or registration is not required of executive housekeepers, though it is something many seek. It is often considered a measure of professional success. The International Executive Housekeepers Association, among other institutions, offers two designations: certified executive housekeeper and registered executive housekeeper. Qualified individuals earn these designations by fulfilling educational requirements through a certificate program, a self-study program, or a college degree program.

High school juniors and seniors who are interested in working in the hospitality industry can take advantage of the Educational Institute of the American Hotel and Lodging Association's Lodging

Management Program. The program combines classroom learning with work experience in the hospitality industry. Graduating seniors who pass examinations and work in the lodging industry for at least 30 days receive the certified rooms division specialist designation. Visit http://www.lodgingmanagement.org for more information.

Other Requirements

Executive housekeepers and their assistants need to be good communicators to keep their staffs happy and working well. Motivation is key when working with large cleaning staffs. In a pinch, good managers may help with cleaning duties. "It helps to know what is expected from all employees, at whatever level, firsthand. It gives you credibility, and respect from your staff," says Kay Wireck, executive housekeeper for Bally's Casino and Resort in Las Vegas.

As with most service-oriented jobs, customers' complaints are inevitable. "Some complaints are credible," says Wireck. "Others are not." It is the manager's job to assess the situation and resolve the problem.

EXPLORING

Try to land a job in the field. You won't be hired as an executive housekeeper, but you can land a position in the housekeeping department. This will give you a good chance to learn more about this career firsthand.

An internship at a hotel can give you a taste of the career without the pressures and obligations of a full-time job. Many recruiters pay more attention to former interns than to those with no past affiliation with the hotel.

EMPLOYERS

Housekeeping is needed in every industry, and positions can be found worldwide. However, jobs are clustered in urban or resort areas where there is great demand for large hotels. Larger hotels usually employ a few assistant executive housekeepers who report to the head of the housekeeping department. If you are an executive housekeeper at a smaller motel or inn, chances are your department may consist of only one or two people. Roll up your sleeves and get ready to clean!

STARTING OUT

This position is among the top rungs of the hotel corporate ladder; very few people start their hospitality careers at this level. Most college graduates start out as floor managers or supervisors and move up from there. High school graduates are usually hired for line-level jobs, such as room attendants. A college degree is not always a requirement, but without one, your climb to the top will take much longer. Check with school placement centers, newspaper want ads, and trade magazines, such as *Executive Housekeeping Today* (http://www.ieha. org/publications/currenteht.html), for job openings.

ADVANCEMENT

Executive housekeepers are considered part of the hotel's executive team and are on the same level as the director of food and beverages or the hotel manager. Because executive housekeepers are already at the head of their particular department, advancement possibilities are limited. Promotions are usually to other hotel departments. Kay Wireck says that she has seen many directors of housekeeping advance to higher positions such as that of general manager. "Anyone with the managerial experience of an executive housekeeper can move on," she says. Executive housekeepers are needed in every industry where cleanliness is top priority.

EARNINGS

Overall earnings are affected by experience, level of education, type and size of organization, and number of employees supervised. The U.S. Department of Labor reports that mean annual earnings of managers of hotel housekeeping and janitorial workers were $28,780. Salaries for all types of hotel managers ranged from less than $25,120 to more than $82,510.

As part of the salary package, managers are offered health, dental, and life insurance; pension or 401(k) plans; and hotel and store discounts. Some hotels and resorts offer on-site living quarters, meals, and laundry services. Year-end bonuses of up to 25 percent of their basic salary are sometimes awarded to managers, depending on the employer.

WORK ENVIRONMENT

Executive housekeepers should expect to be on their feet much of their workday. They must perform walk-arounds of the entire hotel property to ensure that all areas are up to par with hotel standards. They also spend time estimating human and material resource needs with other hotel executives, meeting with different suppliers and vendors, and resolving problems with staff.

The hours are long and stressful. Many executive housekeepers work 10 or more hours a day in order to touch base with all three work shifts. Some weekend and holiday work can be expected, depending on the business demands.

OUTLOOK

The *Occupational Outlook Handbook* reports that employment for all lodging managers—including executive housekeepers—will grow about as fast as the average for all occupations through 2016. Despite this prediction, job prospects for hotel housekeeping executives should remain healthy. Several key factors, among them more international business travel; rising personal incomes; continued growth of the two-income family; and increased emphasis on leisure time and travel, contribute to the need for hotels and qualified people to maintain them. Even with a slower economy, chances are housekeeping will be last on the list for budget trimming. Without the reputation of a clean house, no hotel has a chance for success.

One downside to this occupation, and to the department in general, is the public's perception. Housekeeping is considered by many as very basic work and is often looked down upon. Certification, education, and standardization efforts are helping to give this field the more professional image it deserves.

FOR MORE INFORMATION

For information on careers in hotel management, contact
American Hotel and Lodging Association
1201 New York Avenue, NW, Suite 600
Washington, DC 20005-3931
Tel: 202-289-3100
Email: info@ahla.com
http://www.ahla.com

For information on scholarships and the hospitality industry, contact
American Hotel and Lodging Educational Foundation
1201 New York Avenue, NW, Suite 600
Washington, DC 20005-3931
Tel: 202-289-3180
http://www.ahlef.org

For information on internships, scholarships, and certification requirements, contact
Educational Institute of the American Hotel and Lodging
Association
800 North Magnolia Avenue, Suite 300
Orlando, FL 32803-3271
Tel: 800-752-4567
Email: eiinfo@ahla.com
http://www.ei-ahla.org

For a list of school programs, contact
International Council on Hotel, Restaurant, and Institutional
Education
2810 North Parham Road, Suite 230
Richmond, VA 23294-4422
Tel: 804-346-4800
Email: info@chrie.org
http://chrie.org

For information on certification, contact
International Executive Housekeepers Association
1001 Eastwind Drive, Suite 301
Westerville, OH 43081-3361
Tel: 800-200-6342
Email: excel@ieha.org
http://www.ieha.org

Industrial Traffic Managers

QUICK FACTS

School Subjects
Business
Mathematics

Personal Skills
Communication/ideas
Leadership/management

Work Environment
Primarily indoors
Primarily one location

Minimum Education Level
High school diploma

Salary Range
$16,970 to $73,080 to
$120,000+

Certification or Licensing
Voluntary

Outlook
More slowly than the average

DOT
184

GOE
07.01.01, 09.08.01

NOC
0713

O*NET-SOC
11-3071.01, 43-5071.00

OVERVIEW

Industrial traffic managers, sometimes known as *logistics managers*, handle the booking, billing, claims, and related paperwork for the safe and efficient movement of cargo by air, water, truck, or rail. They analyze the costs of different forms of transport and calculate the shipping rates for customers. There are approximately 89,000 transportation, storage, and distribution managers employed in the United States. Shipping, receiving, and traffic clerks hold about 769,000 jobs.

HISTORY

As the modes of transportation have improved over the centuries, so have the means of transporting freight from place to place. Businesses can now choose from among many alternatives—air, water, truck, or rail—to determine the best method for sending their goods. They want to find the method that will be the most efficient, economical, and reliable arrangement for each particular type of cargo. The job industrial traffic managers perform has helped add organization and efficiency to an increasingly complex process.

With the rise of mass production techniques in the 20th century, manufacturers have been able to produce more products than ever before. A company may produce hundreds of thousands of products each year, and each must reach its ultimate destination, the consumer. The vast numbers of products have created a need for people who specialize in seeing that products are packed, shipped, and received properly and efficiently. Today's industrial traffic managers make

74

use of the latest technological innovations to coordinate the shipping and receiving of products worldwide.

THE JOB

Industrial traffic managers direct and coordinate workers who document, classify, route, and schedule outgoing freight and who verify and reship incoming freight at warehouses and other work sites. They also quote rates and give other information to customers and handle customer complaints about damaged, missing, or overcharged goods. Some traffic managers decide which method of transportation of goods is best. They investigate different means of transportation and then make their decisions based on efficiency and cost. Computers have made the traffic manager's job much easier. In order to make important judgments, traffic managers must make distance and rate calculations that can be done easily and quickly with computers. Computer programs, with their ability to analyze cost-effectiveness, can also help traffic managers decide on the most efficient means of transporting goods.

Traffic agents contact industrial and commercial firms to solicit freight business. These workers call on prospective shippers to explain the advantages of using their company's services. They quote tariff rates, schedules, and operating conditions, such as loading or unloading practices. When an agreement is reached, the traffic agent may also serve as liaison between the shipper and the carrier, help to settle complaints, or follow up on the handling of special goods, such as live animals, delicate equipment, or perishable goods. *Traffic clerks* keep records of incoming and outgoing freight by recording the destination, routing, weight, and tariffs. These workers may also be required to keep records of damaged freight and clients' claims of overcharge. *Shipping services sales representatives* perform similar work for parcel-delivery businesses.

Rate supervisors analyze rates and routes in an effort to find ways to reduce transportation costs. They supervise the work of *traffic-rate clerks,* who determine the rates that a transportation company will charge for shipping cargo of various kinds. *Freight rate analysts* also analyze rates, along with current and proposed government regulations, to determine how the transportation company should revise its rates and practices. These analysts also compile the shipping company's rate manual.

REQUIREMENTS

High School

Many jobs are available to high school graduates, especially with smaller companies, and part-time and summer employment is often available to high school students. You can prepare for a career as an industrial traffic manager by taking courses in economics, mathematics, science, and business administration.

Postsecondary Training

If you are interested in advancing to positions of greater responsibility, you are strongly advised to have at least some postsecondary education. More and more companies have begun to require one to two years of college education for entry into this field, especially when seeking employees interested in making a career with their company. Many community and junior colleges offer traffic and transportation curricula to prepare workers for employment as traffic agents and clerks. Some institutions combine course work with on-the-job experience in programs that lead to an associate's degree or a certificate of completion.

Certification and Licensing

The American Society of Transportation and Logistics offers the certified in transportation and logistics designation to applicants who are active members of the society and who have a four-year undergraduate degree or three years of professional experience. Applicants must pass exams in the following areas: general management principles and techniques, transportation economics and management, logistics management, and international transportation and logistics. They must also pass two of the following elective exam modules: creative component, logistics analysis, supply chain management, and logistics and supply chain strategy.

Other Requirements

Traffic agents and clerks implement the detailed transportation plans or programs that others have developed, as well as communicate these plans to others. To do this, you must be skilled in both verbal and written communication. You must be responsible, dependable, and exacting with details. You must also be able to work easily with numerical data. Basic computer skills are often required for tracking the flow of goods.

EXPLORING

The best opportunity for experience in this field would be a part-time or summer job with a transportation company or a local moving company in a clerical capacity or as a truck helper. In these positions, you would be able to observe the work and responsibilities of traffic agents as well as talk with agents about their positions.

Work-experience programs provided by many companies permit you to get established with an employer as well as obtain valuable experience. You can also contact employers directly through letters of application.

EMPLOYERS

Industrial traffic managers work for all kinds of companies that oversee the transportation of their goods and materials. Traffic agents work for companies that specialize in transportation.

STARTING OUT

Entry-level shipping and receiving positions generally do not require a high degree of educational achievement. Many positions are open to high school graduates, particularly in smaller companies. Management positions, however, are increasingly being filled by graduates of two-year college programs. Therefore, one of the best ways to find an entry-level position as an industrial traffic manager is to work with the career services office of the community or technical

A Day On the Job

According to Ohio State University's 2007 *Survey of Career Patterns in Logistics,* logistics managers reported that they spent their workday doing the following tasks:

- Traffic management: 27.1 percent
- Warehousing: 16.2 percent
- General management: 12.6 percent
- Procurement: 9.2 percent
- Inventory management: 8.2 percent
- Manufacturing logistics: 7.4 percent
- Customer service: 6.9 percent
- Global management: 6.6 percent
- Forecasting: 5.8 percent

college at which you studied. You can also check newspaper want ads for job openings.

ADVANCEMENT

Many paths for advancement exist in this field. For example, someone entering the field as a rate and claims clerk might eventually be promoted to a position as a rate analyst. A routing clerk could be promoted to terminal cargo manager, and a company representative could advance to the position of traffic manager.

EARNINGS

Starting salaries depend greatly on the applicant's level of education, college experience, other relevant work experience, and the degree of responsibility of the position. According to the U.S. Department of Labor, transportation, storage, and distribution managers had median annual earnings of $73,080 in 2006. The lowest paid 10 percent earned less than $43,180 annually. The most experienced industrial traffic managers, often those with a master's degree in business, earn $120,000 or more a year. Shipping, receiving, and traffic clerks earned salaries that ranged from less than $16,970 to more than $50,590 in 2006, according to the U.S. Department of Labor.

Fringe benefits vary widely, depending on the type and size of the company, although most will include vacations and holiday pay, health insurance plans, and in some cases, tuition reimbursement plans.

WORK ENVIRONMENT

Because of the diverse characteristics of each particular mode of transportation, it is difficult to make a general statement about working conditions. Some positions consist of outdoor work, others are almost exclusively indoors, and some are combinations of the two. The hours may be long or shift work may be required since some terminals operate around the clock and certain cargoes must be dispatched as soon as they arrive. Some positions, however, require only regular hours with weekends off.

OUTLOOK

Large and medium-sized companies are increasingly using computers to store and retrieve records. Computerized conveyor systems, robotics, and trucks, as well as scanners, are increasing productivity and eliminating the need for large numbers of workers. Traffic management can never be completely computerized, however. Managers will still be needed to arrange and oversee shipments before they go out and when they arrive. As a result, employment of industrial traffic managers is expected to grow about as fast as the average for all occupations over the next decade, according to the U.S. Department of Labor. Traffic clerks will be more affected by automation as most firms attempt to save money by using computerized tracking systems. Employment for these workers will grow more slowly than the average for all occupations through 2016.

FOR MORE INFORMATION

For information on certification, contact
American Society of Transportation and Logistics
1400 Eye St., NW, Suite 1050
Washington, DC 20005-2209
Tel: 202-580-7270
Email: info@astl.org
http://www.astl.org

For information on college programs and to read the online publication Careers in Logistics, *visit the CSCMP's Web site.*
Council of Supply Chain Management Professionals (CSCMP)
333 East Butterfield Road, Suite 140
Lombard, IL 60148-6016
Tel: 630-574-0985
Email: cscmpadmin@cscmp.org
http://www.cscmp.org

Internet Executives

QUICK FACTS

School Subjects
Business
Computer science

Personal Skills
Communication/ideas
Leadership/management

Work Environment
Primarily indoors
One location with some
travel

Minimum Education Level
Bachelor's degree

Salary Range
$60,800 to $101,580 to
$179,236+

Certification or Licensing
Voluntary

Outlook
Faster than the average

DOT
N/A

GOE
09.01.01, 10.01.01, 13.01.01

NOC
0611

O*NET-SOC
11-1011.00, 11-1011.02,
11-1021.00, 11-3021.00,
11-3031.01

OVERVIEW

Internet executives plan, organize, direct, and coordinate the operations of businesses that engage in commerce over the Internet. These upper-level positions include presidents, chief operating officers, executive vice presidents, chief financial officers, chief information officers, and regional and district managers. The majority of Internet executives are employed in large companies in urban areas.

HISTORY

Since the early 1990s, online business, often called e-commerce, has been extended to virtually every industry. Advertising, distance education programs, sales, banking, tax filing, Web conferencing, bill payment, and online auctions are just a few of the business outlets in which the Internet has profoundly played a role. Companies that have developed a Web presence in these industries, either in addition to or as a replacement to a brick-and-mortar business, need management executives to run their online business dealings just as a normal business needs a CEO. This is the job of Internet executives.

THE JOB

All businesses have specific goals and objectives that they strive to meet, such as making a certain profit or increasing the client base by a certain amount. Executives devise strategies and formulate policies to ensure that these objectives are met. In today's business world, many companies that first began as brick-and-mortar businesses now have a presence on the Internet.

Additionally, many new companies, known as dot-coms, are found only on the Internet. At both types of companies, Internet executives are the professionals who devise ways to meet their companies' objectives—making sales, providing services, or developing a customer base, for example—as they relate to the Internet.

Like executives in traditional companies, Internet executives have a wide range of titles and responsibilities. The positions include president, chairman, chief executive officer (who is sometimes the same person as the president or chairman), chief operating officer, chief financial officer, chief information officer, executive vice presidents, and the board of directors. *Presidents, chairmen,* and *chief executive officers (CEOs)* at companies with an Internet presence are leaders of the companies. They plan business objectives and develop policies to coordinate operations between divisions and departments and establish procedures for attaining objectives. They may review activity reports and financial statements to determine progress and revise operations as needed. They also direct and formulate funding for new and existing programs within their organizations. Public relations play a big part in the lives of Internet executives as they deal with executives and leaders from other countries or organizations, and with customers, employees, and various special interest groups.

Chief operating officers, or *COOs,* at dot-coms and other companies with an Internet presence are typically responsible for the day-to-day operations of the company. They may work to increase their companies' client base, improve sales, and develop operational and personnel policies. Depending on the type of business, other duties a COO may have include heading departments, such as marketing, engineering, or sales. Usually the COO directly reports to the top executive whether it is the CEO, chairman, or president. COOs typically have years of experience working in their industry and may also have worked at their particular company for years, moving up the corporate ranks while gaining knowledge about their companies' products and markets. Additionally, they have extensive knowledge of Internet capabilities and technologies available that will help their companies reach goals.

Some companies have an *executive vice president* who directs and coordinates the activities of one or more departments, depending on the size of the organization. In very large organizations, the duties of executive vice presidents may be highly specialized; for example, they may oversee the activities of business managers of marketing, sales promotion, purchasing, finance, personnel training, industrial relations, administrative services, data processing, property management, transportation, or legal services. In smaller organizations, an executive vice president might be responsible for a number of these departments. Executive vice presidents also assist the CEO in formulating and administering the organization's policies and developing its long-range goals. Executive vice presidents may serve as members of management committees on special studies.

Dot-coms and other companies with a presence on the Internet may also have a *chief financial officer* or *CFO*. In small firms, the CFO is usually responsible for all financial management tasks, such as budgeting, capital expenditure planning, cash flow, and various financial reviews and reports. In larger companies, the CFO may oversee financial management departments to help other managers develop financial and economic policy and oversee the implementation of these policies.

Chief information officers, or *CIOs,* are responsible for all aspects of their company's information technology. They use their knowledge of technology and business to determine how information technology can best be used to meet company goals. This may include researching, purchasing, and overseeing set-up and use of technology systems, such as Intranet, Internet, and computer networks. These managers sometimes take a role in implementing a company's Web site. (For more information on this career, see the article Chief Information Officers.)

Management information systems directors oversee computer and information systems for an entire company. They often report to the chief information officer. They may manage an organization's employee help desk, recommend hardware and software upgrades, and ensure the security and availability of information technology services.

Chief technology officers evaluate and recommend new technologies that will help their organization reduce costs and increase revenue. They often report to the chief information officer.

In companies that have several different locations, managers may be assigned to oversee specific geographic areas. For example, a large retailer with facilities all across the nation may have a Midwest manager, a Southwest manager, a Southeast manager, a Northeast manager, and a Northwest manager. In the case of Internet companies, whose territory is not limited by geographical boundaries, managerial responsibilities may be assigned by product or client type instead.

All of these executive and management positions may be available at large companies, while the responsibilities of several of these positions may be combined into one role at smaller companies. Internet executives may work in any of these positions for companies that do business exclusively online or traditional businesses that also have an online presence. The common denominator among these executives is that they are all involved to some extent with figuring out how to use the Internet to enhance the capabilities and profitability of their businesses.

Rob Linxweiler, a consultant to a number of Internet companies in the Chicago area, says, "A downside of the industry is that sometimes it's hard to measure success on a daily or even weekly basis. We may accomplish two or three major projects per year, and those are the milestones by which we judge ourselves. It's possible to get mired in the day-to-day and fail to see the larger picture."

Linxweiler is quick to point out that there are many positives to an Internet executive's job, including working with interesting people. He also adds, "The work may not always be fascinating, but the technologies available can be used in some creative ways to overcome obstacles. I like to apply my creativity to problem solving."

Involvement in Internet commerce adds a new dimension for the consideration of executives. While most executives don't get directly involved in the day-to-day operation of the technology that drives their Internet business, an understanding of the technologies at work is crucial to the performance of their jobs. Executives will likely have to work directly with technology experts, so proficiency with the relevant technologies is a necessity. The combination of technological and business expertise Internet executives have makes these individuals among the most sought-after in the executive job market.

REQUIREMENTS
High School
The educational background of Internet executives varies as widely as the nature of their diverse responsibilities. Many have a bachelor's degree in computer science, information management, information technology, information security, business administration, or a liberal arts field such as economics or communications. If you are interested in a management career dealing with the Internet, you should plan on going to college after high school. Take a college preparatory curriculum, including classes in science, history, and government. Be sure to take as many computer science classes as possible so that you have a basic understanding of the technology that is available. Because an executive must communicate with a wide range of people, take as many English classes as possible to hone your communication skills. Speech classes are another way to improve these skills. Courses in mathematics and business are also excellent

choices to help you prepare for this career. A foreign language may also be helpful in preparing for today's global business market.

Postsecondary Training

Internet executives often have a college degree in a subject that pertains to the department they direct or the organization they administer. For example, chief executive officers may have business administration degrees, chief financial officers often have accounting degrees, chief information officers often have computer science degrees, and directors of research and development often have engineering or science degrees. All Internet executives are expected to have experience with the information technology that applies to their field. While in college, you should keep up with your computer studies in addition to deciding what type of work interests you. Are you drawn to sales and marketing, for example, or does the actual manufacturing of a product interest you? A good way to find out is to get some hands-on experience through an internship or summer job. Your college career services office should be able to help you locate such a position with a business or organization that appeals to you.

Graduate and professional degrees are common among executives. Many executives in administrative, marketing, financial, and manufacturing activities have a master's degree in business administration. Executives in highly technical manufacturing and research activities often have a master's degree or doctorate in a technical or scientific discipline.

Certification and Licensing

Voluntary computer- and Internet-related certifications are available from professional associations such as the Institute for Certification of Computing Professionals and the Institute of Certified Professional Managers. These designations are helpful in proving your abilities to an employer. The more certifications you have, the more you have to offer.

Other Requirements

There are a number of personal characteristics that make a successful executive, depending upon the specific responsibilities of the position. An executive who manages other employees should have good communication and interpersonal skills. Rob Linxweiler advises, "Work on your communication skills. There is a surprising level of ambiguity in the technological arena, and the ability to say what you mean and be understood is crucial." He adds, "Hands-on experience with some technologies is also very important. The technologies change rapidly. It's not really relevant which particular system you have experience with, but an understanding of the basic processes and rules by which computer technologies operate is extremely important."

The ability to delegate work and think on your feet is often crucial in executive business management. A certain degree of organization is important, since executives often manage many different tasks simultaneously. Other traits considered important for top executives are intelligence, decisiveness, intuition, creativity, honesty, loyalty, and a sense of responsibility. Finally, successful executives should be interested in staying abreast of new developments in their industry and technology.

EXPLORING

To explore your interest in the computer and technology aspect of this work, take every opportunity to work with computers. Surf the Web to visit sites of businesses and organizations and find out what services they offer. Improve your computer skills by joining a users group, setting up your own Web page, and taking extra computer classes at a local community center or tech school.

To get experience as an executive, start with your own interests. Whether you're involved in drama, sports, school publications, or a part-time job, there are managerial and executive duties associated with any organized activity. Look for ways in which you can be involved with planning, scheduling, managing other workers or volunteers, fund-raising, or budgeting. Contact a local business executive—the best source would be one whose company also has a Web site—and ask for an information interview during which you can talk with him or her about this career. Some schools or community organizations arrange "job-shadowing," where interested young people can spend part of a day following selected employees to see what their job is like. Joining Junior Achievement (http://www.ja.org) is another excellent way to get involved with local businesses and learn about how they work. Finally, get a part-time or summer job at a local business to get hands-on experience working in an office environment. Although your job may only be that of cashier, you'll be able to see how the business is organized and run. You may also find a manager or executive there who can act as a mentor and give you advice.

EMPLOYERS

General managers and executives hold 2.2 million jobs in the United States, according to the U.S. Department of Labor. These jobs are found in every industry; however, 75 percent of these jobs are in the service industry—which is heavily involved in the Internet.

Virtually every business in the United States offers executive and managerial positions. Obviously, the larger the company is, the more executive and managerial positions it is likely to have. In addition, companies that do business in larger geographical territories are likely to have more executive and managerial positions than those with smaller territories. Businesses with an Internet presence are the norm in today's market. Almost all large retail businesses have some sort of presence on the World Wide Web, and they find their Web site an essential part of their customer contact program for both sales and marketing. Besides working at large retail businesses, Internet executives may work in such areas as not-for-profit organizations, small start-up companies, and corporate consulting firms.

STARTING OUT

Executive positions are not entry-level jobs. Generally, those interested in becoming Internet executives start with a college degree and gain a significant amount of work experience. After you have decided what industry you are interested in, your college career services office should be able to help you locate your first job. Many companies also send representatives to college campuses to interview graduating students as potential hires. You may also want to attend recruitment and job fairs to find job openings. In addition, a past internship or summer work experience may provide you with contacts that lead to employment. You should research the field you are interested in to find out what might be the best point of entry.

After you have gained some work experience you may want to consider returning to school for a graduate degree. Alternatively, you may be able to work your way up through your organization's management levels. Some organizations have executive management trainee programs available to their employees; other companies may pay for an employee's graduate schooling as long as the employee continues to work for the company. Many executives have master's degrees in business administration, although higher degrees in computer science and related technology fields are becoming more common.

Once you have considerable training and management experience, you can move into an executive level position by directly applying to corporate management. In addition, some executive search and placement firms specialize in job hunting for those involved with the Internet. *Digital agents,* specialists who work only with those seeking technology jobs, may also be a good source of employment leads.

Hiring standards for technology executives are still evolving, but it's clear that simply being well acquainted with the technologies is not enough. You will need significant experience in both business management and technology to meet the requirements of most of these positions.

ADVANCEMENT

Most business management and top executive positions are filled by experienced lower-level managers and executives who display valuable managerial traits, such as leadership, self-confidence, creativity, motivation, decisiveness, and flexibility. Rob Linxweiler says, "Good interpersonal skills are a must. Patience, enthusiasm, and the ability to listen to employees are indispensable skills that are often underrated. The ability to make good decisions and act on them is also vital. These are the building blocks of a strong leader, which is the most important thing an executive can be."

Advancement in smaller firms may come more slowly, while promotions may occur more quickly in larger firms. Advancement may be accelerated by participating in different kinds of educational programs available for managers. These are often paid for by the employer. Managers who take company training programs broaden their knowledge of company policy and operations. Training programs sponsored by industry and trade associations and continuing education courses taken at colleges and universities can familiarize managers with the latest developments in management techniques. In recent years, large numbers of middle managers were laid off as companies streamlined operations. An employee's proven commitment to improving his or her knowledge of the business's field and computer information systems is important in establishing a reputation as a top professional.

Business managers may advance to executive or administrative vice president. Vice presidents may advance to peak corporate positions, such as president or chief executive officer. Sometimes executives go on to establish their own firms.

Many CEOs are moving toward the role of chairman and away from day-to-day operations to focus on higher-level, visionary strategy. The ability to understand and implement solutions based on Internet technologies is essential at this level.

Regardless of the industry, the advancement path of executives at Internet companies is limited only by their interest, abilities, and willingness to work hard.

EARNINGS

Salary levels for Internet executives vary substantially, depending upon their level of responsibility, length of service, and the type, size, and location of the organization for which they work. Top-level executives in large firms can earn much more than their counterparts in small firms. Also, salaries in large metropolitan areas tend to be higher than those in smaller cities.

Computerworld reported the following average salaries (including bonuses) by specialty for Internet executives in 2007: chief information officers, $179,236; chief technology officers, $153,041; and directors of information technology, $111,377.

According to the U.S. Department of Labor, computer and information systems managers had median annual earnings of $101,580 in 2006. Salaries ranged from less than $60,800 to more than $129,250.

Benefit and compensation packages for Internet executives are usually excellent and may include stock awards and options, cash incentives in addition to bonuses, company-paid insurance premiums, use of company cars, club memberships, expense accounts, and generous retirement benefits.

Top executives at successful Internet companies see few limits to their earnings potential; salaries into the millions of dollars are not uncommon for CEOs and other key executives.

WORK ENVIRONMENT

Internet executives work in comfortable offices near the departments they direct. Top executives at established companies may have spacious, lavish offices with comfortable desks and chairs, PCs, phones, and even personal support staff. They may enjoy such privileges as having executive dining rooms, company cars, club memberships, and liberal expense accounts.

Executives often travel between the company's various offices at the national, regional, or local levels. Top executives may travel to meet with executives in other corporations, both within the United States and abroad. Meetings and conferences sponsored by industries and associations occur regularly and provide invaluable opportunities to meet with peers and keep up with the latest developments. In large corporations, job transfers between the parent company and its local offices or subsidiaries are common, so executives must be prepared to move for their work.

Executives often work long hours under intense pressure to meet corporate goals. A typical workweek might consist of 55 to 60 hours at the office. Some executives, in fact, spend up to 80 hours working each week. These long hours limit time available for family and leisure activities, but the financial rewards can be great.

OUTLOOK

Employment of Internet executives is expected to grow faster than the average over the next several years as Internet businesses continue to grow and new companies are formed. The demand will be high for candidates with strong managerial skills and a solid understanding of computer and Internet technology. Education and experience will also count for a lot. Many job openings will be the result of promotions, company expansions, or executives leaving their positions to start their own businesses.

The employment outlook for executives is closely tied to the overall economy. In times when the economy is good, businesses expand both in terms of their output and the number of people they employ. This creates a need for more executives. In economic downturns, businesses often lay off employees and cut back on production, which lessens the need for executives.

There were many highly publicized dot-com failures in the early 2000s. Many experts predict that in the next few years, 80 to 90 percent of dot-coms will either close or be acquired by other companies. The statistics, however, are not likely to deter new Web businesses, especially small businesses that are able to find niche markets, anticipate trends, adapt to market and technology changes, and plan for a large enough financial margin to turn a profit. Traditional brick-and-mortar businesses will also have to implement dot-com marketing plans in order to compete and survive. Analysts anticipate that business-to-business e-commerce will become much more important than business-to-consumer transactions.

FOR MORE INFORMATION

For news about management trends, conferences, and seminars, visit the association's Web site
American Management Association
1601 Broadway
New York, NY 10019-7434

Tel: 877-566-9441
Email: customerservice@amanet.org
http://www.amanet.org

For information on certification, contact
Institute for Certification of Computing Professionals
2350 East Devon Avenue, Suite 115
Des Plaines, IL 60018-4610
Tel: 800-843-8227
Email: office@iccp.org
http://www.iccp.org

For information on certification, contact
Institute of Certified Professional Managers
James Madison University
MSC 5504
Harrisonburg, VA 22807-0001
Tel: 800-568-4120
http://cob.jmu.edu/icpm

For information on programs that teach students about free enterprise and business and information on local chapters, contact
Junior Achievement
One Education Way
Colorado Springs, CO 80906-4477
Tel: 719-540-8000
Email: newmedia@ja.org
http://www.ja.org

For general information on management careers, contact
National Management Association
2210 Arbor Boulevard
Dayton, OH 45439-1506
Tel: 937-294-0421
Email: nma@nma1.org
http://www.nma1.org

There are a number of magazines covering the topics of the Internet, computers, and business. Many are available in print form and online. For a sampling of such magazines, check out the following Web sites
Computerworld
http://www.computerworld.com

Information Week
http://www.internetwk.com

InfoWorld
http://www.infoworld.com

PCWorld
http://www.pcworld.com

Wired
http://www.wired.com

Internet Store Managers and Entrepreneurs

QUICK FACTS

School Subjects
Business
Computer science

Personal Skills
Leadership/management
Technical/scientific

Work Environment
Primarily indoors
Primarily one location

Minimum Education Level
Bachelor's degree

Salary Range
$0 to $25,000 to $60,000+

Certification or Licensing
Voluntary (certification)
Required by certain states
(licensing)

Outlook
Faster than the average

DOT
N/A

GOE
N/A

NOC
N/A

O*NET-SOC
N/A

OVERVIEW

Internet store managers and entrepreneurs use the exciting technology of the Internet to sell products or services. They may research the marketability of a product or service, decide on what product or service to sell, organize their business, and set up their storefront on the Web. Numerous small business owners who sell a limited number of products or a specific service have found the Internet a great place to begin their business venture because start-up costs may be less than for traditional businesses. Internet entrepreneurs run their own businesses. Internet store managers are employed by Internet entrepreneurs and stores.

HISTORY

The Internet became a popular sales tool in the 1990s, and continues to grow today. Although many dot-com companies failed in the early 2000s, Internet sales remain an integral part of our economy. Online sales managers have been listed on *U.S. News & World Report*'s Top 20 Hot Job Tracks.

In 2002, lawmakers and tax officials from 30 states agreed to enter a voluntary pact to collect online sales tax. According to the *Washington Post*, this action was taken partially in response to regular "bricks-and-mortar" stores who complained that online retailers had an advantage.

More and more revenue is generated online each year, and some Internet stores, such as Amazon.com, have had tremendous success in this field. As the Internet continues to grow in popularity and importance, more consumers will be exposed to Internet stores on a daily basis. This will create a strong demand for Internet managers and entrepreneurs to research and market potential products and services, as well as manage businesses and employees.

THE JOB

In spite of the failure of many high-profile dot-coms in the early 2000s, many online businesses have continued to survive and thrive. These e-tailers have adapted to the constantly changing technology, economic climate, business trends, and consumer demands, instead of concentrating on fast growth and offering the lowest prices. Reports by research firm Jupiter Communications show that consumers are using Internet stores to do comparison shopping, and a significant number of consumers research products online before buying them at traditional stores.

Because of the vastness of the Internet, the role of an Internet store manager or entrepreneur can vary as much as the numerous Web sites on the Internet. Expert opinion on what makes one Web site or one business more successful than another differs, too. E-commerce is a new and relatively unexplored field for entrepreneurs. But, because most entrepreneurs have innovative and creative natures, this uncertainty and uncharted territory is what they love.

Like traditional entrepreneurs, Internet entrepreneurs must have strong business skills. They come up with ideas for an Internet product or service, research the feasibility of selling this product or service, decide what they need to charge to make a profit, determine how to advertise their business, and even arrange for financing for their business if necessary. In addition, Internet entrepreneurs typically have computer savvy and may even create and maintain their own sites.

Some entrepreneurs may choose to market a service, such as Web site design, to target the business-to-business market. Other Internet entrepreneurs may decide to market a service, such as computer dating, to target the individual consumer market. Still others may develop a "virtual store" on the Internet and sell products that target businesses or individual consumers.

Internet stores vary in size, items for sale, and range of products. Smaller Internet stores, for example, may market the work done by a single craftsperson or businessperson. Many large Internet stores focus on selling a specific product or line of products. As some of these stores have grown, they have diversified their merchandise. Amazon.com is one such example. Originally, a small, online bookstore, the company now sells music CDs, videos, jewelry, toys and housewares, along with books. Other Internet stores, such as those of Eddie Bauer and Sears, may be extensions of catalog or traditional brick-and-mortar stores. These large companies are generally so well established that they can employ Internet store managers to oversee the virtual store.

Many Internet businesses begin small, with one person working as the owner, manager, Webmaster, marketing director, and accountant, among other positions. John Axne of Chicago, Illinois, took on all these responsibilities when he developed his own one-person business designing Web sites for small companies and corporations. "Having my own business allows me more creative freedom," says Axne. The successful Internet entrepreneur, like the successful traditional entrepreneur, is often able to combine his or her interests with work to fill a niche in the business world. "It's a great fit for me," Axne explains. "I have a passion for computers and a love of learning. This business allows me to sell myself and my services." Dave Wright of Venice, California, is also an Internet entrepreneur and Web site designer. He, too, combined his interests with computer skills to start his business. "I had a strong interest in art," he says. "I simply married my art and graphic art experience with computers."

Those who want to start their own businesses on the Web must be very focused and self-motivated. Just like any other entrepreneur, they always need to keep an eye on the competition to see what products and services as well as prices and delivery times others offer. While Internet entrepreneurs do not need to be computer whizzes, they should enjoy learning about technology so that they can keep up with new developments that may help them with their businesses. Internet entrepreneurs must also be decision makers, and many are drawn to running their own businesses because of the control it offers. "I'm a control freak," Wright admits. "This way I can oversee every aspect of my job."

The typical day of the Internet store manager or entrepreneur will depend greatly on the size and scope of the company where he or she works.. Someone who works for a large company that also has a Web site store, for example, may meet with company department heads to find out about upcoming sales or products that should be heavily advertised on the Web site. They may do research about the store use and report their findings to company managers. They may work on the site itself, updating it with new information.

The Internet entrepreneur also has varied responsibilities that depend on his or her business. Wright notes, "No two projects and no two days are alike." An entrepreneur may spend one day working with a client to determine the client's needs and the next day working on bookkeeping and advertising in addition to working on a project. Most entrepreneurs, however, enjoy this variety and flexibility.

While the Internet world is appealing to many, there are risks for those who start their own businesses. "The Internet changes so rapidly that in five years it may be entirely different," Wright says. "That's why I started a business that simply sells services and didn't require a major investment. It is a business that I can get into and out of quickly if I find it necessary. There is no product, per se, and no inventory." Despite uncertainties, however, Web stores continue to open and the number of Internet store managers and entrepreneurs continues to grow.

REQUIREMENTS

High School

If you are considering becoming an Internet store manager or entrepreneur, there are a number of classes you can take in high school to help prepare you for these careers. Naturally, you should take computer science courses to give you a familiarity with using computers and the Web. Business and marketing courses will also be beneficial. Also, take mathematics, accounting, or bookkeeping classes because, as an entrepreneur, you will be responsible for your company's finances. Take history classes to learn about economic trends and psychology classes to learn about human behavior. A lot of advertising and product promotion has a psychological element. Finally, take plenty of English classes. These classes will help you develop your communication skills—skills that will be vital to your work as a store manager or business owner.

Postsecondary Training

Although there are no specific educational requirements for Internet store managers or entrepreneurs, a college education will certainly enhance your skills and chances for success. Like anyone interested in working for or running a traditional business, take plenty of business, economics, and marketing and management classes. Your education should also include accounting or bookkeeping classes. Keep up with computer and Internet developments by taking computer classes. Some schools offer certificates and degrees in e-commerce. Many schools have undergraduate degree programs in business or business administration, but you can also enter this field with other degrees. Dave Wright, for example, graduated with a degree from art school, while John Axne has degrees in biomedical engineering and interactive media.

Certification or Licensing

While there are no specific certifications available for Internet store managers and entrepreneurs, professional associations such as the Institute for Certification of Computing Professionals and the Institute of Certified Professional Managers offer voluntary management-related certifications to industry professionals. These designations are helpful in proving your abilities to an employer. The more certifications you have, the more you have to offer.

Licenses may be required for running a business, depending on the type of business. Since requirements vary, you will need to check with local and state agencies for regulations in your area.

Other Requirements

Internet entrepreneurs and store managers must have the desire and initiative to keep up on new technology and business trends. Because they must deal with many different people in various lines of work, they need to be flexible problem solvers and have strong communication skills. Creativity and insight into new and different ways of doing business are qualities that are essential for an entrepreneur to be successful. In addition, because the Internet and e-commerce are relatively new and the future of Internet businesses is uncertain, those who enter the field are generally risk-takers and eager to be on the cutting edge of commerce and technology. Dave Wright notes, "This is not a job for someone looking for security. The Internet world is always changing. This is both exciting and scary to me as a businessperson. This is one career where you are not able to see where you will be in five years."

EXPLORING

There are numerous ways in which you can explore your interest in the computer and business worlds. Increase your computer skills and find out how much this technology interests you by joining a computer users group or club at your high school or your community. Access the Internet frequently on your own to observe different Web site designs and find out what is being sold and marketed electronically. What sites do you think are best at promoting products and why? Think about things from a customer's point of view. How easy are the sites to access and use? How are the products displayed and accessed? How competitive are the prices for goods or services?

Make it a goal to come up with your own ideas for a product or service to market on the Web, then do some research. How difficult would it be to deliver the product? What type of financing would be involved? Are there other sites already providing this product or service? How could you make your business unique?

Talk to professionals in your community about their work. Set up information interviews with local business owners to find out what is involved in starting and running a traditional business. Your local chamber of commerce or the Small Business Administration may have classes or publications that would help you learn about starting a business. In addition, set up information interviews with computer consultants, Web site designers, or Internet store managers or owners. How did they get started? What advice do they have? Is there anything they wish they had done differently? Where do they see the future of e-commerce going?

If your school has a future business owners club, join this group to meet others with similar interests. For hands-on business experience, get a part-time or summer job at any type of store in your area. This work will give you the opportunity to deal with customers (who can sometimes be hard to please), work with handling money, and observe how the store promotes its products and services.

EMPLOYERS

Internet store managers may work for an established traditional business or institution that also has a Web site dealing with products and services. The manager may also work for a business that only has a presence on the Web or for an Internet entrepreneur. Entrepreneurs are self-employed, and sometimes they may employ people to work under them. Some Internet entrepreneurs may be hired to begin a business for someone else.

STARTING OUT

Professionals in the field advise those just starting out to work for someone else to gain experience in the business world before beginning their own business. The Internet is a good resource to use to find employment. There are many sites that post job openings. Local employment agencies and newspapers and trade magazines also list job opportunities. In addition, your college career services office should be able to provide you with help locating a job. Networking with college alumni and people in your computer user groups may also provide job leads.

Top 10 Online Department Stores

1. Amazon.com
2. Walmart.com
3. Target.com
4. Sears.com
5. JCPenney.com
6. Overstock.com
7. QVC.com
8. Macys.com
9. Kohls.com
10. Kmart.com

Source: Hitwise, December 2007 (by number of visits)

ADVANCEMENT

Advancement opportunities depend on the business, its success, and the individual's goals. Internet entrepreneurs or store managers who are successful may enter other business fields or consulting. Alternatively, they may advance to higher-level management positions or other larger Internet-based businesses. Some entrepreneurs establish a business and then sell it only to begin another business venture. The Internet world is constantly changing because of technological advancements. This state of flux means that a wide variety of possibilities are available to those working in the field. "There is no solid career path in the Internet field," says Dave Wright. "Your next career may not even be developed yet."

EARNINGS

Income for Internet store managers and entrepreneurs is usually tied to the profitability of the business. Internet store managers who work for established traditional businesses are typically salaried employees of the company. Internet entrepreneurs who offer a service may be paid by the project. Entrepreneurs are self-employed and their income will depend on the success of the business. Those just starting out may actually have no earnings, while those with a business that has been existence for several years may have annual earnings between $25,000 and $50,000. Some in the field may earn much more than this amount. John Axne estimates that those who have good technical skills and can do such things as create the database program for a Web site may have higher salaries, in the $60,000 to $125,000 range.

Entrepreneurs are almost always responsible for their own medical, disability, and life insurance. Retirement plans must also be self-funded and self-directed. Internet store managers may or may not receive benefits.

WORK ENVIRONMENT

Internet entrepreneurs and store managers may work out of a home or private office. Some Internet store managers may be required to work on site at a corporation or small business.

The entrepreneur must deal with the stresses of starting a business, keeping it going, dealing with deadlines and customers, and coping with problems as they arise. They must also work long hours to develop and manage their business venture; many entrepreneurs work over 40 hours a week. Evening or weekend work may also be required, for both the entrepreneur and the store manager.

In addition, these professionals must spend time researching, reading, and checking out the competition in order to be informed about the latest technology and business trends. Their intensive computer work can result in eyestrain, hand and wrist injuries, and back pain.

OUTLOOK

Online commerce is a very new and exciting field with tremendous potential, and it is likely that growth will continue over the long term. However, it is important to keep in mind that the failure rate for new businesses, even traditional ones, is fairly high. Some experts predict that in the next few years, 80 to 90 percent of dot-coms either will close or be acquired by other companies. The survivors will be small businesses that are able to find niche markets, anticipate trends, adapt to market and technology changes, and plan for a large enough financial margin to turn a profit. Analysts also anticipate that the amount of business-to-business e-commerce will surpass business-to-consumer sales.

Internet managers and entrepreneurs with the most thorough education and experience and who have done their research will have the best opportunities for success. For those who are adventurous and interested in using new avenues for selling products and services, the Internet offers many possibilities.

FOR MORE INFORMATION

For information about the information technology industry and e-commerce, contact
Information Technology Association of America
1401 Wilson Boulevard, Suite 1100
Arlington, VA 22209-2318
Tel: 703-522-5055
http://www.itaa.org

For information on certification, contact
Institute for Certification of Computing Professionals
2350 East Devon Avenue, Suite 115
Des Plaines, IL 60018-4610
Tel: 800-843-8227
http://www.iccp.org

For information on certification, contact
Institute of Certified Professional Managers
James Madison University
MSC 5504
Harrisonburg, VA 22807-0001
Tel: 800-568-4120
http://icpm.biz

The Small Business Administration offers helpful information on starting a business. For information on state offices and additional references, visit its Web site.
Small Business Administration
409 Third Street, SW
Washington, DC 20416-0001
Tel: 800-827-5722
Email: answerdesk@sba.gov
http://www.sba.gov

Check out the following online magazine specializing in topics of interest to entrepreneurs
Entrepreneur.com
http://www.entrepreneur.com

Lawn and Gardening Service Owners

OVERVIEW

Lawn and gardening service owners maintain the lawns of residential and commercial properties. They cut grass and shrubbery, clean yards, and treat grass with fertilizer and insecticides. They may also landscape, which involves the arrangement of lawns, trees, and bushes. There are about 1.5 million people employed in the grounds maintenance industry. Nearly 25 percent of landscapers, groundskeepers, and nursery workers are self-employed.

HISTORY

If you've ever visited or seen photographs of the Taj Mahal in India or Versailles in France, then you've seen some elaborate examples of the lawns and gardens of the world. For as long as people have built grand palaces, they have designed lawns and gardens to surround them. Private, irrigated gardens of ancient Egypt and Persia were regarded as paradise with their thick, green vegetation and cool shade. In the 16th century, Italians kept gardens that wound about fountains, columns, and steps. The English developed the "cottage-style" gardens to adhere to the natural surroundings. Early American gardens, such as those surrounding Monticello in Virginia, were inspired by this English style.

The English also inspired the Georgian style of house design in the 18th century that caught on across Europe and America. Rows of houses down city blocks were designed as units, their yards hidden

School Subjects
Agriculture
Technical/shop

Personal Skills
Following instructions
Mechanical/manipulative

Work Environment
Primarily outdoors
Primarily multiple locations

Minimum Education Level
High school diploma

Salary Range
$23,940 to $50,000 to $100,000+

Certification or Licensing
Voluntary (certification)
Required by certain states (licensing)

Outlook
Faster than the average

DOT
408

GOE
03.01.02

NOC
N/A

O*NET-SOC
37-1012.00, 37-1012.01

behind the houses and away from the streets. Lawn care as a business blossomed with the growth of population and home ownership between the Civil War and World War I. The sport of golf also became popular among the rich at this time, spurring further development of lawn care products and machinery. Since World War II, many people now hire lawn maintenance professionals to keep up and improve the look of their personal lawns and gardens.

THE JOB

Lawn and gardening businesses may choose to offer only a few services, such as lawn mowing and hedge clipping. However, some businesses offer a large number of services, from simple cleaning to the actual design of the yard. Some lawn services specialize in organic lawn care. They rely on natural fertilizers and applications to control insects and lawn diseases instead of applying toxic chemicals to treat lawns.

When working for private homeowners, lawn and gardening services do yard work once or twice a week for each client. They arrive at the residence with equipment, such as a push or riding mower, an aerator, and a blower vac. Workers cut the grass and "weed-eat," trimming the weeds at the edges of the houses and fences. They also apply fertilizer and insecticide to the lawn to keep the grass healthy and use an aerator to run over the yard to make holes in the topsoil and allow more airflow.

Lawn and gardening service owners participate in all aspects of the business, including the labor. They plant grass seed in areas where there is little growth, and use blowers to blow leaves and other debris from the yard, sidewalks, and driveway. Lawn services are often called in after storms and other natural disasters to clean up and repair lawns.

"There are a lot of little services you can throw in to keep you busy," says Sam Morgan, who operates a lawn care service in Dallas, Texas. He does general lawn maintenance for residential yards and some rental properties. "Having some rental property can be good," he says. "It's year-round work. But it can also be dirty work; you have to pick up a lot of trash."

In addition to mowing yards and weed-eating, Morgan assists with planting flower beds, cleaning house gutters, and some light tree work. Tree care involves the pruning and trimming of branches. Lawn and gardening services may need to remove dead or unwanted trees before planting new ones. They may also offer landscaping services, offering advice on arranging the lawn. Service owners assist in positioning trees, bushes, fountains, flower beds, and lighting. They may also put up wood or metal fencing, and install sprinkler systems.

"I started the business on a shoestring," Morgan says. "But I learned early that you have to have good equipment." He now owns a commercial mower that can handle 200 yards a week.

Lawn and gardening service owners have other responsibilities than just lawn and garden care. As owners, they are responsible for the business end of the service. In order to stay in business, owners must balance the budget, collect on accounts, repair or replace equipment when necessary, order supplies, and, depending on the size of the business, hire and manage other employees.

In addition to working on the demanding yard work, Morgan spends much of his time attending to business details, such as keeping tax records, making phone calls, and preparing estimates and bills.

REQUIREMENTS

High School
Take agriculture, shop, and other courses that will help you gain familiarity with the machinery, fertilizers, and chemicals used in lawn maintenance. Agriculture courses will also teach you about different grasses and plants, and how to care for them. Joining associations such as the National FFA Organization (formerly the Future Farmers of America) and 4-H can give you additional experience with horticulture. Business and accounting courses are also useful to learn about record keeping, budgeting, and finances.

Postsecondary Training
After high school, you can learn about lawn maintenance on the job, either by assisting someone with an established lawn care business, or by taking on a few residential customers yourself. Though a college degree is not necessary, lawn and gardening service owners benefit from advanced courses such as small business management and finance to help run their business.

Certification or Licensing
Certification is not required, but many lawn and garden service owners choose to earn professional certifications from the Professional Landcare Network. The network offers the following certification designations: certified landscape professional, certified landscape technician-interior, certified landscape technician-exterior, certified turfgrass professional, certified turfgrass professional-cool season lawns, and certified ornamental landscape professional. Depending

A lawn service owner applies pesticide to a customer's lawn. *(Dennis MacDonald, Unicorn Stock Photos)*

on the certification, applicants must pass a multiple-choice examination or a hands-on field test.

Most states require lawn care professionals who apply pesticides to be licensed. This usually involves passing a written examination on the safe use and disposal of toxic chemicals.

Other Requirements

As entrepreneurs, lawn and gardening service owners need to have people skills and be self-motivated to successfully promote their own business and attract clients.

"I'm a good salesman," Sam Morgan says. He also emphasizes the need to be committed to doing a quality job for every customer. Service owners should have an eye for detail to notice all the areas where lawns need work. They must also be in fairly good health to withstand the hard labor that the job calls for, often during the heat of the summer.

EXPLORING

If you've made some extra money mowing lawns for your neighbors, then you're already familiar with many of the aspects of a lawn care service. Walking behind a power mower during the hottest days of the year may make you miserable, but early experience in keeping your next-door neighbor's lawn looking nice is a great opportunity for self-employment. Other sources for potential clients are private homeowners, apartment complex communities, golf courses, and parks. Look into volunteer and part-time work with botanical gardens, greenhouses, and park and recreation crews.

Opportunities to learn how to care for a lawn and garden are no further than your own backyard. Experiment with planting and maintaining different varieties of flowers, shrubs, or trees. Chances are, you'll gain valuable experience and your parents will thank you!

In addition to getting dirt under your fingernails, you can also explore the lawn and garden services by reading magazines and books on lawn and garden care. Cable television stations, such as Home and Garden Television (HGTV), feature programming about gardening.

Every summer, many high school students find reliable work mowing lawns. But many of these students tire of the work early in the summer. Be persistent in seeking out work all summer long. You should also be committed to doing good work; you'll have stiff competition from professional lawn care businesses that offer more services, own commercial machinery, and have extensive knowledge of fertilizers and pesticides. Some lawn care companies also hire students for summer work.

EMPLOYERS

Lawn and gardening service owners work primarily for private homeowners, though they may also contract work with commercial properties. Condos, hotels, apartment complexes, golf courses, sports fields, and parks all require regular lawn service.

Owners who choose to build their own business face challenges such as covering the costs of start up and establishing a client base. To defray these costs and risks, many choose to purchase and operate an existing business. There are a number of franchise opportunities in lawn care that, for a fee, will assist you in promoting your business and building a clientele. Emerald Green Lawn Care, Liqui-Green Lawn Care, and Lawn Doctor are just a few. NaturaLawn of America is a franchise that provides organic-based lawn care.

STARTING OUT

Most lawn and gardening service owners start out working for established services and work their way into positions of management or higher responsibility. A typical entry-level job is that of the landscape service technician. After a few years on the job, promising technicians may be promoted to supervisor positions such as regional or branch managers. According to the Professional Landcare Network, "once a supervisory position is reached, leadership is the key to success." Workers who are organized, show strong leadership, and can make decisions quickly and wisely will have the best chances for promotion and may choose to start up their own business.

However, not all service owners follow this route. Sam Morgan's lawn service was not his first venture into entrepreneurship; he had once owned a number of dry cleaners. After selling the dry cleaners, he went to work for a chemical company. When the company downsized, Morgan was faced with finding a new job. He decided to turn to lawn care.

"I just went to Sears and bought a mower," he says. Since then, he's been able to invest in commercial machinery that can better handle the demands of the work, and he's found a number of ways to increase business. "I bill once a month," he says. "I get more business that way." He's also expanding his service to include some light landscaping, such as shrub work and planting small trees.

Depending on the business, start-up costs can vary. To purchase commercial quality equipment, the initial investment can be between $3,000 and $4,000. Buying into a franchise, however, will cost thousands of dollars more.

ADVANCEMENT

Once lawn and gardening service owners establish their own businesses, advancement can come in the form of expanded services. Some lawn professionals offer equipment and supply sales. With extended services, owners can reach out to a larger body of clients, securing larger contracts with golf courses, cities and local communities, and sports teams.

Sam Morgan currently has one employee, but he hopes for his business to grow more, allowing him to hire others. "I don't want to be doing so much of the physical work," he says.

With additional education, owners can also advance into other areas of lawn care and become contractors or landscape architects.

EARNINGS

Earnings in lawn care depend on a number of factors, such as geographic location, the size of the business, and the level of experience. Lawn care services generally make more money in areas of the country that have mild winters, offering more months of lawn growth and, as a result, requiring more care. The size of the client base also greatly affects earnings. A lawn care professional with a small clientele may make less than $20,000 a year, while the owner of a franchise lawn care company with a number of contracts and a large staff can make over $100,000.

According to 2006 data from the U.S. Department of Labor, first-line supervisors/managers of landscaping, lawn service, and groundskeeping workers made an average of $17.93 an hour (or $37,300 annually). Salaries ranged from less than $23,940 to $60,930 or more annually. The Professional Landcare Network offers the following summary of earnings potential for management positions: first-level supervisors, $35,000; branch managers, $50,000 or more; regional managers, $60,000s; and successful owners, $100,000 or more.

WORK ENVIRONMENT

To many, working on a lawn or garden is relaxing, and the opportunity to work outdoors during pleasant days of spring and summer is enjoyable. However, the work can also be exhausting and strenuous. Lawn and gardening service owners fully involved in the labor of the business may have to lift heavy equipment from trucks, climb trees, and do a lot of walking, kneeling, and bending on the job. Depending on the nature of the business, service owners may have to exercise caution when handling harmful chemicals used in pesticides. In addition, they have to deal with a loud work environment because machinery such as lawn mowers, weed eaters, and blow vacs can be very noisy.

One benefit of owning a business is the ability to create a flexible work schedule. "Most likely," Sam Morgan says, "during the spring and summer, you can make plenty of money. There's plenty of work to be done." But some of that work may be in the hottest days of the summer, or on rainy days. With your own service, you can arrange to work regular weekday hours, or you can schedule weekends.

OUTLOOK

The benefits of a nice lawn aren't just aesthetic; a well-kept lawn can increase property value and provide a safe place for children to play. According to the National Gardening Association, more than 34.5 million U.S. households spent $44.7 billion on professional lawn and landscape services in 2006.

This spending promises a good future for lawn care services. The sale of lawn care products is expected to grow as more houses are built and more people recognize the importance of quality lawn care. The Environmental Protection Agency promotes the environmental benefits of a healthy lawn, emphasizing that healthy grass is not only attractive, but controls dust and pollens, provides oxygen, and improves the quality of groundwater. More people now recognize that a nice lawn can increase home value by as much as 20 percent, according to studies.

Technological developments will also aid the industry. With better, more economical equipment, lawn care professionals can do more specialized work in less time, allowing them to keep their service fees low.

FOR MORE INFORMATION

For general information about franchising, specific franchise opportunities, and Introduction to Franchising, *contact the IFA.*
International Franchise Association (IFA)
1501 K Street, NW, Suite 350
Washington, DC 20005-1412
Tel: 202-628-8000
Email: ifa@franchise.org
http://www.franchise.org

To further explore the agriculture industry and for information on student chapters, contact
National FFA Organization
6060 FFA Drive
PO Box 68960
Indianapolis, IN 46268-0960
Tel: 317-802-6060
http://www.ffa.org

For information on certification, careers, internships, and student membership, contact
Professional Landcare Network
950 Herndon Parkway, Suite 450
Herndon, VA 20170-5528
Tel: 800-395-2522
Email: info@landcarenetwork.org
http://www.landcarenetwork.org/cms/home.html

Management Analysts and Consultants

OVERVIEW

Management analysts and consultants analyze business or operating procedures to devise the most efficient methods of accomplishing work. They gather and organize information about operating problems and procedures and prepare recommendations for implementing new systems or changes. They may update manuals outlining established methods of performing work and train personnel in new applications. There are approximately 678,000 management analysts and consultants employed in the United States.

HISTORY

A number of people in business began experimenting with accepted management practices after the industrial revolution. For example, in the 1700s, Josiah Wedgwood applied new labor- and work-saving methods to his pottery business and was the first to formulate the concept of mass-producing articles of uniform quality. He believed the manufacturing process could be organized into a system that would use, and not abuse, the people harnessed to it. He organized the interrelationships between people, material, and events in his factory and took the time to reflect upon them. In short, he did in the 18th century what management analysts and consultants do today.

Frederick W. Taylor was the creator of the "efficiency cult" in American business. Taylor invented the world-famous "differential piecework" plan, in which a productive worker could significantly

QUICK FACTS

School Subjects
Business
Computer science
Speech

Personal Skills
Communication/ideas
Leadership/management

Work Environment
Primarily indoors
Primarily multiple locations

Minimum Education Level
Bachelor's degree

Salary Range
$39,840 to $68,050 to
$250,000+

Certification or Licensing
Voluntary

Outlook
Much faster than the average

DOT
161

GOE
13.02.04

NOC
1122

O*NET-SOC
13-1111.00

increase take-home pay by stepping up the pace of work. Taylor's well-publicized study of the Midvale Steel plant in Pennsylvania was the first time-and-motion study. It broke down elements of each part of each job and timed it, and it was therefore able to quantify maximum efficiency. He earned many assignments and inspired James O. McKinsey, in 1910, to found a firm dealing with management and accounting problems.

Today, management analysts and consultants are thriving. As technological advances lead to the possibility of dramatic loss or gain in the business world, many executives feel more secure relying on all the specialized expertise they can find.

THE JOB

Management analysts and consultants are called in to solve any of a vast array of organizational problems. They are often needed when a rapidly growing small company needs a better system of control over inventories and expenses.

The role of the consultant is to come into a situation in which a client is unsure or inexpert and to recommend actions or provide assessments. There are many different types of management analysts and consultants. In general, they all require knowledge of general management, operations, marketing, logistics, materials management and physical distribution, finance and accounting, human resources, electronic data processing and systems, and management science.

Management analysts and consultants may be called in when a major manufacturer must reorganize its corporate structure when acquiring a new division. For example, they assist when a company relocates to another state by coordinating the move, planning the new facility, and training new workers.

The work of management analysts and consultants is quite flexible—it varies from job to job. In general, management analysts and consultants collect, review, and analyze data, make recommendations, and assist in the implementation of their proposals. Some projects require several consultants to work together, each specializing in a different area. Other jobs require the analysts to work independently.

Public and private organizations use management analysts for a variety of reasons. Some organizations lack the resources necessary to handle a project. Other organizations, before they pursue a particular course of action, will consult an analyst to determine what resources will be required or what problems will be encountered. Some companies seek outside advice on how to resolve organizational problems that have already been identified or to avoid troublesome problems that could arise.

Firms providing consulting practitioners range in size from solo practitioners to large international companies employing hundreds of people. The services are generally provided on a contract basis. A company will choose a consulting firm that specializes in the area that needs assistance, and then the two firms negotiate the conditions of the contract. Contract variables include the proposed cost of the project, staffing requirements, and the deadline.

After getting a contract, the analyst's first job is to define the nature and extent of the project. He or she analyzes statistics, such as annual revenues, employment, or expenditures. He or she may also interview employees and observe the operations of the organization on a day-to-day basis.

The next step for the analyst is to use his or her knowledge of management systems to develop solutions. While preparing recommendations, he or she must take into account the general nature of the business, the relationship of the firm to others in its industry, the firm's internal organization, and the information gained through data collection and analysis.

Once they have decided on a course of action, management analysts and consultants usually write reports of their findings and recommendations and present them to the client. They often make formal oral presentations about their findings as well. Some projects require only reports; others require assistance in implementing the suggestions.

REQUIREMENTS

High School

High school courses that will give you a general preparation for this field include business, mathematics, and computer science. Management analysts and consultants must pass on their findings through written or oral presentations, so be sure to take English and speech classes, too.

Postsecondary Training

Employers generally prefer to hire management analysts and consultants with a master's degree in business or public administration, or at least a bachelor's degree and several years of appropriate work experience. Many college majors provide a suitable education for this occupation because of the diversity of problem areas addressed by management analysts and consultants. These include many areas in the computer and information sciences, engineering, business and management, education, communications, marketing and distribution, and architecture and environmental design.

When hired directly from school, management analysts and consultants often participate in formal company training programs. These programs may include instruction on policies and procedures, computer systems and software, and management practices and principles. Regardless of their background, most management analysts and consultants routinely attend conferences to keep abreast of current developments in the field.

Certification and Licensing
The Institute of Management Consultants, in cooperation with the Association of Internal Management Consultants, offers the certified management consultant designation to those who pass an examination and meet minimum educational and experience criteria. Certification is voluntary, but may provide an additional advantage to job seekers.

Other Requirements
Management analysts and consultants are often responsible for recommending layoffs of staff, so it is important that they learn to deal with people diplomatically. Their job requires a great deal of tact, enlisting cooperation while exerting leadership, debating their points, and pointing out errors. Consultants must be quick thinkers and able to refute objections with finality. They also must be able to make excellent presentations.

A management analyst must also be unbiased and analytical, with a disposition toward the intellectual side of business and a natural curiosity about the way things work best.

EXPLORING
The reference departments of most libraries include business areas that will have valuable research tools such as encyclopedias of business consultants and "who's who" of business consultants. These books should list management analysis and consulting firms across the country, describing their annual sales and area of specialization, like industrial, high tech, small business, and retail. After doing some research, you can call or write to these firms and ask for more information.

For more general business exploration, see if your school has a business or young leaders club. If there is nothing of the sort, you may want to explore Junior Achievement, a nationwide association that connects young business-minded students with professionals in the field for mentoring and career advice. Visit http://www.ja.org for more information.

EMPLOYERS

About 27 percent of the 678,000 management analysts and consultants in the United States are self-employed. Federal, state, and local governments employ many of the others. The Department of Defense employs the majority of those working for the federal government. The remainder work in the private sector for companies providing consulting services. Although management analysts and consultants are found throughout the country, the majority are concentrated in major metropolitan areas.

STARTING OUT

Most government agencies offer entry-level analyst and consultant positions to people with bachelor's degrees and no work experience. Many entrants are also career changers who were formerly mid- and upper-level managers. With 27 percent of the practicing management consultants self-employed, career changing is a common route into the field.

Anyone with some degree of business expertise or an expert field can begin to work as an independent consultant. The number of one- and two-person consulting firms in this country is well over 100,000. Establishing a wide range of appropriate personal contacts is by far the most effective way to get started in this field. Consultants have to sell themselves and their expertise, a task far tougher than selling a tangible product the customer can see and handle. Many consultants get their first clients by advertising in newspapers, magazines, and trade or professional periodicals. After some time in the field, word-of-mouth advertising is often the primary method of attracting new clients.

ADVANCEMENT

A new consultant in a large firm may be referred to as an *associate* for the first couple of years. The next progression is to *senior associate*, a title that indicates three to five years' experience and the ability to supervise others and do more complex and independent work. After about five years, the analyst who is progressing well may become an *engagement manager* with the responsibility to lead a consulting team on a particular client project. The best managers become *senior engagement managers*, leading several study teams or a very large project team. After about seven years, those who excel will be considered for appointment as *junior partners* or *principals*. Partnership involves responsibility for marketing the firm and leading client projects. Some may be promoted to senior partnership or *director,* but few people successfully run this full course. Management analysts and consultants with entrepreneurial ambition may open their own firms.

EARNINGS

Salaries and hourly rates for management analysts and consultants vary widely, according to experience, specialization, education, and employer. In 2006, management analysts and consultants had median annual earnings of $68,050, according to the U.S. Department of Labor. The lowest 10 percent earned less than $39,840, and the highest 10 percent earned more than $128,330.

Many consultants can demand between $400 and $1,000 per day. Their fees are often well over $40 per hour. Self-employed management consultants receive no fringe benefits and generally have to maintain their own office, but their pay is usually much higher than salaried consultants. They can make more than $2,000 per day or $250,000 in one year from consulting just two days per week.

Typical benefits for salaried analysts and consultants include health and life insurance, retirement plans, vacation and sick leave, profit sharing, and bonuses for outstanding work. All travel expenses are generally reimbursed by the employer.

WORK ENVIRONMENT

Management analysts and consultants generally divide their time between their own offices and the client's office or production facility. They can spend a great deal of time on the road.

Most management analysts and consultants work at least 40 hours per week plus overtime depending on the project. The nature of consulting projects—working on location with a single client toward a specific goal—allows these professionals to immerse themselves in their work. They sometimes work 14- to 16-hour days, and six- or seven-day workweeks can be fairly common.

While self-employed, consultants may enjoy the luxury of setting their own hours and doing a great deal of their work at home; the trade-off is sacrificing the benefits provided by the large firms. Their livelihood depends on the additional responsibility of maintaining and expanding their clientele on their own.

Although those in this career usually avoid much of the potential tedium of working for one company all day, every day, they face many pressures resulting from deadlines and client expectations. Because the clients are generally paying generous fees, they want to see dramatic results, and the management analyst can feel the weight of this pressure.

OUTLOOK

Employment of management analysts is expected to grow much faster than the average for all occupations through 2016, according to the U.S. Department of Labor (USDL). Industry and government agencies are expected to rely more and more on the expertise of these professionals to improve and streamline the performance of their organizations. Many job openings will result from the need to replace personnel who transfer to other fields or leave the labor force.

Competition for management consulting jobs will be strong. Employers can choose from a large pool of applicants who have a wide variety of educational backgrounds and experience. The challenging nature of this job, coupled with high salary potential, attracts many. A graduate degree, experience and expertise in the industry, as well as a knack for public relations, are needed to stay competitive.

Trends that have increased the growth of employment in this field include advancements in information technology and e-commerce, the growth of international business, and fluctuations in the economy that have forced businesses to streamline and downsize.

The USDL predicts that opportunities will be best at very large consulting firms that have expertise in international business and in smaller firms that focus on providing consulting services in specific areas such as biotechnology, engineering, information technology, health care, marketing, and human resources.

FOR MORE INFORMATION

For industry information, contact the following organizations
American Institute of Certified Public Accountants
1211 Avenue of the Americas
New York, NY 10036-8775
Tel: 212-596-6200
http://www.aicpa.org

American Management Association
1601 Broadway
New York, NY 10019-7434

Tel: 877-566-9441
http://www.amanet.org

Association of Management Consulting Firms
380 Lexington Avenue, Suite 1700
New York, NY 10168-0002
Tel: 212-551-7887
Email: info@amcf.org
http://www.amcf.org

For information on certification, contact
Association of Internal Management Consultants
824 Caribbean Court
Marco Island, FL 34145-3422
Tel: 239-642-0580
Email: info@aimc.org
http://www.aimc.org

For information on certification, contact
Institute of Management Consultants
2025 M Street, NW, Suite 800
Washington, DC 20036-3309
Tel: 800-221-2557
Email: office@imcusa.org
http://www.imcusa.org

Manufacturing Supervisors

OVERVIEW

Manufacturing supervisors, sometimes known as *industrial production managers,* monitor employees and their working conditions and effectiveness in production plants and factories. They ensure that work is carried out correctly and on schedule by promoting high product quality and output levels. In addition to balancing the budget and other bookkeeping duties, supervisors maintain employee work schedules, train new workers, and issue warnings to workers who violate established rules. Manufacturing managers in various industries hold approximately 157,000 jobs.

HISTORY

Manufacturing has been through many technological developments, from innovations in fuel-powered machinery to the assembly line. As these processes became more complex, no single worker could be responsible for the production of particular items. Manufacturing became a long process involving many workers' contributions. If one worker caused a defect in the product, it was not always easy to track down the source of the problem. The role of the supervisor emerged as a means of keeping track of the work of numerous employees involved in the production process, allowing production to run smoothly.

THE JOB

The primary roles of manufacturing supervisors are to oversee their employees and ensure the effectiveness of the production process.

They are responsible for the amount of work and the quality of work being done by the employees under their direction. Supervisors make work schedules, keep production and employee records, and plan on-the-job activities. Their work is highly interpersonal. They not only monitor employees, but also guide workers in their efforts and are responsible for disciplining and counseling poor performers as well as recommending valuable employees for raises and promotions. They also make sure that safety regulations and other rules and procedures are being followed.

In monitoring production and output levels, manufacturing supervisors must keep in mind the company's limitations, such as budgetary allowances, time constraints, and any workforce shortages. They must be realistic about the abilities of their employees and set production schedules accordingly. Supervisors may use mathematical calculations and test various production methods to reach high production levels while still maintaining the quality of the product.

Manufacturing supervisors may be employed by small companies, such as custom furniture shops, or large industrial factories, such as automotive plants. Supervisors answer to company managers, who direct them on production goals and set budgets. Another important part of the supervisor's job is to act as a liaison between factory workers and company managers who are in charge of production. Supervisors announce new company policies and plans to the workers in their charge and report to their managers about any problems they may be having or other important issues. Supervisors also may meet with other company supervisors to discuss progress toward company objectives, department operations, and employee performance. In companies where employees belong to labor unions, supervisors must know and follow all work-related guidelines outlined by labor-management contracts.

REQUIREMENTS
High School
If you are interested in becoming a manufacturing supervisor, take high school courses in business, math, and science to prepare for the demands of the job. In order to balance the budget and determine production schedules, supervisors often use mathematical computations. They also use computers to do much of their paperwork, so take any available classes to become familiar with word processing and spreadsheet programs.

A manufacturing supervisor *(far left)* examines pill bottles for defects with two of his employees in a warehouse. *(William Taufic, Corbis)*

Postsecondary Training

Because manufacturing areas differ, there is no single path to a supervisory position. However, most manufacturing supervisors hold a college degree in business administration, management, industrial technology, or industrial engineering. College courses in business, industrial relations, math, and computer applications help to familiarize prospective supervisors with the many responsibilities they will have to handle. Interpersonal skills are also highly valuable so classes in public relations and human resource management are also important.

Many supervisors obtain graduate degrees to become more marketable to employers or for a better chance of advancing within a company. As manufacturing processes have become more complex, advanced degrees in business administration, engineering, or industrial management are more and more common among those in higher-level positions.

Certification and Licensing

Voluntary certification is offered by several professional associations, including the Association for Operations Management and the American Society for Quality. Contact these organizations for more information.

Other Requirements

Manufacturing supervisors deal with many people on a highly personal level. They must direct, guide, and discipline others, so you should work on developing strong leadership qualities. You will also need good communication skills and the ability to motivate people and maintain morale.

EXPLORING

To better gauge your interest and expand your knowledge about manufacturing careers, ask your school's guidance counselor for advice on setting up a tour of a local production factory or plant. At the factory or plant, you might be able to talk to workers about their jobs or at least see the environment in which they work. Simply reading more about the field of manufacturing and its many different employment opportunities is also a good way to explore this career. Visit your local library or surf the Internet for recent articles and information.

A summer or part-time job in an office or retail setting can give you business experience and expose you to management practices. Depending on the job and industry, perhaps you might even be promoted to an assistant manager position.

EMPLOYERS

There are approximately 157,000 manufacturing supervisors working all over the United States, but the majority of jobs are located in highly industrial areas. Whether it is in a small production facility or a large factory or plant, supervisors are needed to oversee all manufacturing processes. The major employment areas are industrial machinery and equipment, semiconductor and other electronic components, plastics products, transportation equipment, motor vehicle parts, electronic and electrical equipment, metal instruments and related products, printing and related services, and food industries. A small number of these managers are self-employed.

STARTING OUT

Many supervisors enter their jobs by moving up from factory worker positions. They may also apply for supervisory positions from out-

Books to Read

Camenson, Blythe. *Careers for Self-Starters & Other Entrepreneurial Types.* 2d ed. New York: McGraw-Hill, 2004.

Christie, Sally. *Vault Guide to International Careers.* New York: Vault Inc., 2004.

Crittendon, Robert. *The New Manager's Starter Kit.* New York: AMACOM Books, 2007.

Halloran, Ed. *Careers in International Business.* 2d ed. New York: McGraw-Hill, 2003.

McGraw-Hill. *Resumes for Business Management Careers.* 3d ed. New York: McGraw-Hill, 2006.

Shoup, Kate. *What Can You Do With a Major in Business: Real People. Real Jobs. Real Rewards.* Hoboken, N.J.: CliffsNotes, 2005.

Stair, Lila B., and Leslie Stair. *Careers in Business.* 5th ed. New York: McGraw-Hill, 2005.

side the company. Companies that hire manufacturing supervisors look for experience, knowledge of the job or industry, organizational skills, and leadership abilities. Supervisory positions may be found in classified ads, but for those just looking to get started, part-time or full-time jobs in a factory setting may help provide some experience and familiarity with the work of supervisors.

ADVANCEMENT

In most manufacturing companies, an advanced degree in business management or administration along with accumulated work experience is the best method for advancement into higher level supervisory positions. From the position of supervisor, one may advance to manager or head of an entire manufacturing plant or factory.

EARNINGS

Salaries for manufacturing supervisors vary depending on the factory or plant in which they work, the area of production that they supervise, and their years of experience in the position. The U.S. Department of Labor reports that the median annual salary for manufacturing supervisors was $77,670 in 2006. The lowest 10 percent earned less than $47,230, and the highest 10 percent earned more than $130,680.

Manufacturing supervisors typically receive benefits such as retirement plans, medical and life insurance, and paid holidays and vacations.

WORK ENVIRONMENT

Most supervisors work on the manufacturing or factory floor. They may be on their feet most of the time, which can be tiring, and work near loud and hazardous machines. Supervisors may begin their day early so that they arrive before their workers, and they may stay at work later than their workers. Some may work for plants that operate around the clock and may work overnight shifts, weekends, and holidays. Sometimes the best hours go to those who have been with the company the longest. Plant downsizing and restructuring often leads to fewer supervisors. As a result, manufacturing supervisors may face larger departments to oversee and other increased demands.

OUTLOOK

To some extent, the future of the manufacturing supervisor job depends on the individual industry, whether it be automobiles or food products. In manufacturing as a whole, employment of supervisors is expected to decline through 2016 as fewer supervisors have begun to oversee more workers. Corporate downsizing and the use of computers for tasks such as producing production schedules and budget plans are creating a diminishing need for supervisors. However, there will be a need to replace job-changing or retiring managers. Job candidates with higher levels of education (especially those with an undergraduate engineering degree and a master's degree in business administration, industrial engineering, or industrial management) and related work experience will fare the best in landing a supervisory position.

FOR MORE INFORMATION

For information on workplace trends and management and leadership training, contact
American Management Association
1601 Broadway
New York, NY 10019-7434
Tel: 877-566-9441
http://www.amanet.org

For information on certification, contact
American Society for Quality
PO Box 3005
Milwaukee, WI 53201-3005
Tel: 800-248-1946
http://www.asq.org

Association for Operations Management
5301 Shawnee Road
Alexandria, VA 22312-2317
Tel: 800-444-2742
http://www.apics.org

For general information on manufacturing careers, industry news, and training tools, contact
National Association of Manufacturers
1331 Pennsylvania Avenue, NW
Washington, DC 20004-1790
Tel: 202-637-3000
Email: manufacturing@nam.org
http://www.nam.org

For useful information on manufacturing careers, contact
GetTech.org
http://www.gettech.org

Office Administrators

QUICK FACTS

School Subjects
Business
Mathematics
Speech

Personal Skills
Communication/ideas
Leadership/management

Work Environment
Primarily indoors
Primarily one location

Minimum Education Level
Associate's degree

Salary Range
$26,530 to $43,510 to
$71,340+

Certification or Licensing
Voluntary

Outlook
More slowly than the average

DOT
169

GOE
09.01.01

NOC
1221

O*NET-SOC
11-3011.00, 43-1011.02

OVERVIEW

Office administrators direct and coordinate the work activities of office workers within an office. They supervise office clerks and other workers in their tasks and plan department activities with other supervisory personnel. Administrators often define job duties and develop training programs for new workers. They evaluate the progress of their clerks and work with upper management officials to ensure that the office staff meets productivity and quality goals. Office administrators often meet with office personnel to discuss job-related issues or problems, and they are responsible for maintaining a positive office environment. There are approximately 1.4 million office administrators employed in the United States.

HISTORY

The growth of business since the industrial revolution has been accompanied by a corresponding growth in the amount of work done in offices. Records, bills, receipts, contracts, and other paperwork have proliferated. Phone calls, emails, and other communications have multiplied. Accounting and bookkeeping practices have become more complicated.

The role of the office administrator has also grown over time. In the past, such supervisors were responsible mainly for ensuring productivity and good work from their clerks and reporting information to management. Today, office administrators play a more active part in the operations of busy offices. They are responsible for coordinating the activities of many departments, informing management of departmental performance, and making sure the highly specialized sectors of an office run smoothly and efficiently every day.

THE JOB

As modern technology and an increased volume of business communications become a normal part of daily business, offices are becoming more complicated places in which to work. By directing and coordinating the activities of clerks and other office workers, office administrators are an integral part of an effective organization.

The day-to-day work of office administrators, also known as *office managers*, involves organizing and overseeing many different activities. Although specific duties vary with the type and size of the particular office, all supervisors and managers have several basic job responsibilities. The primary responsibility of the office administrator is to run the office; that is, whatever the nature of the office's business, the office administrator must see to it that all workers have what they need to do their work.

Office administrators are usually responsible for interviewing prospective employees and making recommendations on hiring. They train new workers, explain office policies, and explain performance criteria. Office administrators are also responsible for delegating work responsibilities. This requires a keen understanding of the strengths and weaknesses of each worker, as well as the ability to determine what needs to be done and when it must be completed. For example, if a supervisor knows that one worker is especially good at filing business correspondence, that person will probably be assigned important filing tasks. Office administrators often know how to do many of the tasks done by their subordinates and assist or relieve them whenever necessary.

Office administrators not only train clerical workers and assign them job duties but also recommend increases in salaries, promote workers when approved, and occasionally fire them. Therefore, they must carefully observe clerical workers performing their jobs (whether answering the telephones, opening and sorting mail, or inputting computer data) and make positive suggestions for any necessary improvements. Managers who can communicate effectively, both verbally and in writing, will be better able to carry out this kind of work. Motivating employees to do their best work is another important component of an office administrator's responsibilities.

Office administrators must be very good at human relations. Differences of opinion and personality clashes among employees are inevitable in almost any office, and the administrator must be able to deal with grievances and restore good feelings among the staff. Office administrators meet regularly with their staff, alone and in groups, to discuss and solve any problems that might affect people's job performance.

Planning is a vital and time-consuming portion of the job responsibilities of office administrators. Not only do they plan the work of subordinates, they also assist in planning current and future office space needs, work schedules, and the types of office equipment and supplies that need to be purchased.

Office administrators must always keep their superiors informed as to the overall situation in the clerical area. If there is a delay on an important project, for example, upper management must know the cause and the steps being taken to expedite the matter.

REQUIREMENTS

High School

A high school diploma is essential for this position, and a college degree is highly recommended. You should take courses in English, speech and communications, mathematics, sociology, history, and as many business-related courses, such as typing and bookkeeping, as possible. Knowledge of a wide variety of computer software programs is also very important.

Postsecondary Training

In college, pursue a degree in business administration or at least take several courses in business management and operations. In some cases, an associate's degree is considered sufficient for a supervisory position, but a bachelor's degree will make you more attractive to employers and help in advancement.

Many community colleges and vocational schools offer business education courses that help train office administrators. The American Management Association has certificate programs in several areas, including administrative excellence, human resources, leadership, management excellence, and supervisory excellence. (See contact information at the end of this article.)

Colleges and universities nationwide offer bachelor's degrees in business administration; a few may offer programs targeted to specific industries, such as medical administration or hotel management.

Certification and Licensing

The International Association of Administrative Professionals offers voluntary certification to administrative professionals. Applicants who meet experience requirements and who pass an examination may use the designation, certified administrative professional. The Institute of Certified Professional Managers offers the certified manager designation to applicants who pass examinations that cover the foundations of management, planning and organizing, and leading and controlling.

Other Requirements

Offices can be hectic places. Deadlines on major projects can create tension, especially if some workers are sick or overburdened. Office administrators must constantly juggle the demands of their superiors with the capabilities of their subordinates. Thus, they need an even temperament and the ability to work well with others. Additional important attributes include organizational ability, attention to detail, dependability, and trustworthiness. Since many offices promote administrators from clerical work positions within their organization, relevant work experience is also helpful.

EXPLORING

You can get general business experience by taking on clerical or bookkeeping responsibilities with a school club or other organization. Volunteering in your school office is an ideal introduction to office work. This will allow you to become more familiar with computer programs often used in offices and practice business skills such as opening and sorting mail, answering telephones, and filing documents.

Community colleges and other institutions may offer basic or advanced computer training courses for students of all ages. After high school, you may want to explore work-study programs where you can work part time and gain on-the-job training with local businesses while earning your degree.

EMPLOYERS

Approximately 1.4 million office administrators are employed in the United States. Administrators are needed in all types of offices that have staffs large enough to warrant a manager. The federal government is a major employer of office administrators. Other job opportunities are found in private companies with large clerical staffs, such as banks, telecommunications companies, wholesalers, retail establishments, business service firms, healthcare facilities, schools, and insurance companies.

STARTING OUT

To break into this career, you should contact the personnel offices of individual firms directly. This is especially appropriate if you have previous clerical experience. College career services offices or other job placement offices may also know of openings. You can also locate jobs through help wanted advertisements. Another option is to sign up with a temporary employment service. Working as a "temp" provides the advantage of getting a firsthand look at a variety of office settings and making many contacts.

Often, a firm will recruit office administrators from its own clerical staff. A clerk with potential supervisory abilities may be given periodic supervisory responsibilities. Later, when an opening occurs for an administrator, that person may be promoted to a full-time position.

ADVANCEMENT

Skilled administrators may be promoted to group manager positions. Promotions, however, often depend on the individual's level of education and other appropriate training, such as training in the company's computer system. Firms usually encourage their employees to pursue further education and may even pay for some tuition costs. Supervisory and management skills can be obtained through company training or community colleges and local vocational schools.

Some companies will prepare office clerks for advancement to administrative positions by having them work in several company departments. This broad experience allows the administrator to better coordinate numerous activities and make more knowledgeable decisions.

EARNINGS

According to the U.S. Department of Labor, office administrators earned median annual salaries of $43,510 in 2006. Fifty percent earned between $33,730 and $56,130 a year. The lowest paid 10 percent earned less than $26,530, and the top 10 percent earned more than $71,340.

The size and geographic location of the company and the person's individual skills can be key determinants of earnings. Higher wages will be paid to those who work for larger private companies located in and around major metropolitan areas. Full-time workers also receive paid vacations and health and life insurance. Some companies offer year-end bonuses and stock options.

WORK ENVIRONMENT

As is the case with most office workers, office administrators work an average of 35 to 40 hours a week, although they may also be asked to work overtime. Depending on the company, night, weekend, holiday, or shift work may be expected. Most offices are pleasant places to work. The environment is usually well ventilated and well lighted, and the work is not physically strenuous. The administrator's job can be stressful, however, as it entails supervising a variety of employees with different personalities, temperaments, and work habits.

OUTLOOK

Employment of office administrators is projected to grow more slowly than the average for all occupations through 2016, according to the U.S. Department of Labor. The increased use of data processing and other automated equipment as well as corporate downsizing may reduce the number of administrators in the next decade. However, this profession will still offer good employment prospects because of its sheer size. A large number of job openings will occur as administrators transfer to other industries or leave the workforce for other reasons. Since some clerical occupations will be affected by increased automation, some office administrators may have smaller staffs and be asked to perform more professional tasks.

The federal government should continue to be a good source for job opportunities. Private companies, particularly those with large clerical staffs, such as hospitals, banks, and telecommunications companies, should also have numerous openings. Employment opportunities will be especially good for those who are familiar with the latest computer technology and office equipment.

FOR MORE INFORMATION

For news about management trends, resources on career information and finding a job, and an online job bank, contact
American Management Association
1601 Broadway
New York, NY 10019-7434
Tel: 877-566-9441
http://www.amanet.org

For information on certification, contact
Institute of Certified Professional Managers
James Madison University
MSC 5504
Harrisonburg, VA 22807-0001
Tel: 800-568-4120
http://icpm.biz

For career and certification information, contact
International Association of Administrative Professionals
10502 NW Ambassador Drive
PO Box 20404
Kansas City, MO 64195-0404
Tel: 816-891-6600
Email: service@iaap-hq.org
http://www.iaap-hq.org

For information about programs for students in kindergarten through high school, and information on local chapters, contact
Junior Achievement
One Education Way
Colorado Springs, CO 80906-4477
Tel: 719-540-8000
Email: newmedia@ja.org
http://www.ja.org

For a career information, contact
National Management Association
2210 Arbor Boulevard
Dayton, OH 45439-1506
Tel: 937-294-0421
Email: nma@nma1.org
http://www.nma1.org

Personnel and Labor Relations Specialists

OVERVIEW

Personnel specialists, also known as human resources professionals, formulate policy and organize and conduct programs relating to all phases of personnel activity. Labor relations specialists serve as mediators between employees and the employer. They represent management during the collective-bargaining process when contracts with employees are negotiated. They also represent the company at grievance hearings, required when a worker feels management has not fulfilled its end of an employment contract. There are approximately 868,000 personnel specialists employed in the United States.

HISTORY

The concept of personnel work developed as businesses grew in size from small owner-operated affairs to large corporate structures with many employees. As these small businesses became larger, it became increasingly difficult for owners and managers to stay connected and in touch with all their employees and still run the day-to-day operations of the business. Smart business owners and managers, however, were aware that the success of their companies depended upon attracting good employees, matching them to jobs they were suited for, and motivating them to do their best. To meet these needs, the personnel department was established, headed

QUICK FACTS

School Subjects
Business
Psychology

Personal Skills
Communication/ideas
Leadership/management

Work Environment
Primarily indoors
One location with some
    travel

Minimum Education Level
Bachelor's degree

Salary Range
$26,000 to $52,270 to
    $114,860+

**Certification or
Licensing**
Recommended

Outlook
Faster than the average

DOT
166

GOE
13.01.01, 13.02.01

NOC
1223

O*NET-SOC
11-3040.00, 11-3041.00,
    11-3042.00, 11-3049.00,
    13-1071.00, 13-1071.01,
    13-1071.02, 13-1072.00,
    13-1073.00, 13-1079.00,
    43-4111.00, 43-4161.00

by a specialist or staff of specialists whose job was to oversee all aspects of employee relations.

The field of personnel, or human resources, grew as business owners and managers became more aware of the importance of human psychology in managing employees. The development of more sophisticated business methods, the rise of labor unions, and the enactment of government laws and regulations concerned with the welfare and rights of employees have all created an even greater need for personnel specialists who can balance the needs of both employees and employers for the benefit of all.

The development and growth of labor unions in the late 1700s and early 1800s created the need for a particular kind of personnel specialist—one who could work as a liaison between a company's management and its unionized employees. Labor relations specialists often try to arbitrate, or settle, employer-employee disagreements. One of the earliest formal examples of this sort of arbitration in the United States was the first arbital tribunal created by the New York Chamber of Commerce in 1768. Although arbitration resolutions were often ignored by the courts in the preindustrial United States, by the end of World War I, the court system was overwhelmed by litigation. In 1925, Congress passed the Federal Arbitration Act, which enforced arbitration agreements between employers and employees that were reached without judicial involvement, in order to relieve the burdens placed on the court system by this labor litigation explosion. Today, personnel and labor relations workers are an integral part of the corporate structure to promote and communicate the needs of workers to management.

THE JOB

Personnel and labor relations specialists are the liaison between the management of an organization and its employees. They see that management makes effective use of employees' skills, while at the same time improving working conditions for employees and helping them find fulfillment in their jobs. Most positions in this field involve heavy contact with people, at both management and nonmanagement levels.

Both personnel specialists and labor relations specialists are experts in employer-employee relations, although the labor relations specialists concentrate on matters pertaining to union members. Personnel specialists interview job applicants and select or recommend those who seem best suited to the company's needs. Their choices for hiring and advancement must follow the guidelines for equal employment opportunity and affirmative action established by the federal government. Personnel specialists also plan and maintain programs for wages and salaries, employee benefits, and training and career development.

In small companies, one person often handles all the personnel work. This is the case for Susan Eckerle, human resources manager for Crane Federal Credit Union. She is responsible for all aspects of personnel management for 50 employees who work at three different locations. "I handle all hiring, employee relations counseling, corrective action, administration of benefits, and termination," she says. When Eckerle started working for the credit union, there was no specific human resources department. Therefore, much of her time is spent establishing policies and procedures to ensure that personnel matters run smoothly and consistently. "I've had to write job descriptions, set up interview procedures, and write the employee handbook," she says. "In addition, we don't have a long-term disability plan, and I think we need one. So I've been researching that."

Although Eckerle handles all phases of the human resources process, this is not always the case. The personnel department of a large organization may be staffed by many specialists, including recruiters, interviewers, job analysts, and specialists in charge of benefits, training, and labor relations. In addition, a large personnel department might include *personnel clerks* and *assistants* who issue forms, maintain files, compile statistics, answer inquiries, and do other routine tasks.

Personnel managers and *employment managers* are concerned with the overall functioning of the personnel department and may be involved with hiring, employee orientation, record keeping, insurance reports, wage surveys, budgets, grievances, and analyzing statistical data and reports. *Industrial relations directors* formulate the policies to be carried out by the various department managers.

Of all the personnel specialists, the one who first meets new employees is often the recruiter. Companies depend on *personnel recruiters* to find the best employees available. To do this, recruiters develop sources through contacts within the community. In some cases, they travel extensively to other cities or to college campuses to meet with college placement directors, attend campus job fairs, and conduct preliminary interviews with potential candidates.

Employment interviewers interview applicants to fill job vacancies, evaluate their qualifications, and recommend hiring the most promising candidates. They sometimes administer tests, check references and backgrounds, and arrange for indoctrination and training. They must also be familiar and current with guidelines for equal employment opportunity (EEO) and affirmative action.

In very large organizations, the complex and sensitive area of EEO is handled by specialists who may be called *EEO representatives, affirmative-action coordinators,* or *job development specialists.* These specialists develop employment opportunities and on-the-job training programs for minority or disadvantaged applicants; devise systems or set up representative committees through which grievances can be investigated and resolved as they come up; and monitor corporate practices to prevent possible EEO violations. Preparing and submitting EEO statistical reports is also an important part of their work.

Job analysts are sometimes also called *compensation analysts* and *position classifiers.* They study all of the jobs within an organization to determine job and worker requirements. Through observation and interviews with employees, they gather and analyze detailed information about job duties and the training and skills required. They write summaries describing each job, its specifications, and the possible route to advancement. Job analysts classify new positions as they are introduced and review existing jobs periodically. These job descriptions, or position classifications, form a structure for hiring, training, evaluating, and promoting employees, as well as for establishing an equitable pay system.

Occupational analysts conduct technical research on job relationships, functions, and content; worker characteristics; and occupational trends. The results of their studies enable business, industry, and government to utilize the general workforce more effectively.

Developing and administering the pay system is the primary responsibility of the *compensation manager.* With the assistance of other specialists on the staff, compensation managers establish a wage scale designed to attract, retain, and motivate employees. A realistic and fair compensation program takes into consideration company policies, government regulations concerning minimum wages and overtime pay, rates currently being paid by similar firms and industries, and agreements with labor unions. The compensation manager is familiar with all these factors and uses them to determine the compensation package.

Training specialists prepare and conduct a wide variety of education and training activities for both new and existing employees. Training specialists may work under the direction of an *education and training manager.* Training programs may cover such special areas as apprenticeship programs, sales techniques, health and safety practices, and retraining displaced workers. The methods chosen by training specialists for maximum effectiveness may include individual training, group instruction, lectures, demonstrations, meetings, or workshops, using such teaching aids as handbooks, demonstration models, multimedia programs, and reference works. These specialists also confer with management and supervisors to determine the needs for new training programs or revision of existing ones, maintain records of all training activities, and evaluate the success of the various programs and methods. Training instructors may work under the direction of an education and training manager. *Coordinators of auxiliary personnel* specialize in training nonprofessional nursing personnel in medical facilities.

Training specialists may help individuals establish career development goals and set up a timetable in which to strengthen job-related skills and learn new ones. Sometimes this involves outside study paid for by the company or rotation to jobs in different departments of the organization. The extent of the training program and the responsibilities of the training specialists vary considerably, depending on the size of the firm and its organizational objectives.

Benefits programs for employees are handled by *benefits managers* or *employee-welfare managers*. The major part of such programs generally involves insurance and pension plans. Since the enactment of the Employee Retirement Income Security Act (ERISA), reporting requirements have become a primary responsibility for personnel departments in large companies. The retirement program for state and local government employees is handled by *retirement officers.* In addition to regular health insurance and pension coverage, employee benefit packages have often grown to include such things as dental insurance, accidental death and disability insurance, automobile insurance, homeowner's insurance, profit sharing and thrift/savings plans, and stock options. The expertise of benefits analysts and administrators is extremely important in designing and carrying out the complex programs. These specialists also develop and coordinate additional services related to employee welfare, such as car pools, child care, cafeterias and lunchrooms, newsletters, annual physical exams, recreation and physical fitness programs, and counseling. Personal and financial counseling for employees close to retirement age is growing especially important.

In some cases—especially in smaller companies—the personnel department is responsible for administering the occupational safety and health programs. The trend, however, is toward establishing a separate safety department under the direction of a safety engineer, industrial hygienist, or other safety and health professionals.

Personnel departments may have access to resources outside the organization. For example, *employer relations representatives* promote the use of public employment services and programs among local employers. *Employee-health maintenance program specialists* help set up local government-funded programs among area employers to provide assistance in treating employees with alcoholism or behavioral medical problems.

In companies where employees are covered by union contracts, labor relations specialists form the link between union and management. Prior to negotiation of a collective-bargaining agreement, *labor relations managers* counsel management on their negotiating position and provide background information on the provisions of the current contract and the significance of the proposed changes. They also provide reference materials and statistics pertaining to labor legislation, labor market conditions, prevailing union and management practices, wage and salary surveys, and employee benefit programs. This work requires that labor relations managers be familiar with sources of economic and wage data and have an extensive knowledge of labor law and collective-bargaining trends. In the actual negotiation, the employer is usually represented by the director of labor relations or another top-level official, but the members of the company's labor relations staff play an important role throughout the negotiations.

Specialists in labor relations, or union-management relations, usually work for unionized organizations, helping company officials prepare for collective-bargaining sessions, participating in contract negotiations, and handling day-to-day labor relations matters. A large part of the work of labor relations specialists is analyzing and interpreting the contract for management and monitoring company practices to ensure their adherence to the terms. Of particular importance is the handling of grievance procedures. To investigate and settle grievances, these specialists arrange meetings between workers who raise a complaint, managers and supervisors, and a union representative. A grievance, for example, may concern seniority rights during a layoff. Labor relations disputes are sometimes investigated and resolved by *professional conciliators* or *mediators*. Labor relations work requires keeping up to date on developments in labor law, including arbitration decisions, and maintaining close contact with union officials.

Government personnel specialists do essentially the same work as their counterparts in business, except that they deal with public employees whose jobs are subject to civil service regulations. Much of government personnel work concentrates on job analysis, because civil service jobs are strictly classified as to entry requirements, duties, and wages. In response to the growing importance of training and career development in the public sector, however, an entire industry of educational and training consultants has sprung up to provide similar services for public agencies. The increased union strength among government workers has resulted in a need for more highly trained labor relations specialists to handle negotiations, grievances, and arbitration cases on behalf of federal, state, and local agencies.

REQUIREMENTS

High School

To prepare for a career as a personnel or labor relations specialist, you should take high school classes that will help prepare you for college. A solid background in the basics—math, science, and English—should be helpful in college-level work. You might especially focus on classes that will help you understand and communicate easily with people. Psychology, English, and speech classes are all good choices. Business classes can help you understand the fundamental workings of the business world, which is also important. Finally, foreign language skills could prove very helpful, especially in areas where there are large numbers of people who speak a language other than English.

Postsecondary Training

High school graduates may start out as personnel clerks and advance to a professional position through experience, but such situations are becoming rare. Most employers require personnel specialists and labor relations specialists to have a college degree. After high school, Susan Eckerle attended a four-year college and received a bachelor's degree in retail management, with a minor in psychology. She says that if she were starting over now, however, she would get a degree in human resources instead.

There is little agreement as to what type of undergraduate training is preferable for personnel and labor relations work. Some employers favor college graduates who have majored in human resources, human resources administration, or industrial and labor relations, while others prefer individuals with a general business background. Another opinion is that personnel specialists should have a well-rounded liberal arts education, with a degree in psychology, sociology, counseling, or education. A master's degree in business administration is also considered suitable preparation. Students interested in personnel work with a government agency may find it an asset to have a degree in personnel administration, political science, or public administration.

Individuals preparing for a career as a personnel specialist will benefit from a wide range of courses. Classes might include business administration, public administration, psychology, sociology, political science, and statistics. For prospective labor relations specialists, valuable courses include labor law, collective bargaining, labor economics, labor history, and industrial psychology.

Work in labor relations may require graduate study in industrial or labor relations. While not required for entry-level jobs, a law degree is necessary for those who conduct contract negotiations, and a combination of industrial relations courses and a law degree is especially desirable. For a career as a professional arbitrator, a degree in industrial and labor relations, law, or personnel management is required.

Certification or Licensing

Some organizations for human resources professionals offer certification programs, which usually consist of a series of classes and a test. For example, the International Foundation of Employee Benefits Plans offers the certified employee benefits specialist designation to candidates who complete a series of college-level courses and pass exams on employee benefits plans. Other organizations that offer certification include the American Society for Training and Development, the Society for Human Resource Management, and WorldatWork Society of Certified Professionals. Though voluntary, certification is highly recommended and can improve chances for advancement.

Other Requirements

Personnel and labor relations specialists must be able to communicate effectively and clearly both in speech and in writing and deal comfortably and easily with people of different levels of education and experience. "You've got to be people oriented," says Eckerle. "You have to love people and like working with them. That is huge."

Objectivity and fair-mindedness are also necessary in this job, where you often need to consider matters from both the employee's and the employer's point of view. "Being the liaison between management and employees can put you in a tough spot sometimes," Eckerle says. "You're directly between the two poles, and you have to be able to work with both sides."

These workers cooperate as part of a team; at the same time, they must be able to handle responsibility individually. Eckerle says it is important to be organized because you are often responsible for tracking many different things regarding many different people. "You can't be sloppy in your work habits, because you're dealing with a lot of important information and it all has to be processed correctly," she says.

EXPLORING

If you enjoy working with others, you can find helpful experience in managing school teams, planning banquets or picnics, working in your dean's or counselor's office, or reading books about personnel practices in businesses. You might also contact and interview the personnel director of a local business to find out more about the day-to-day responsibilities of this job. Part-time and summer employment in firms that have a personnel department are very good ways to explore the personnel field. Large department stores usually have personnel departments and should not be overlooked as a source of temporary work.

EMPLOYERS

Personnel specialists hold approximately 868,000 jobs, with close to 90 percent working in the private sector. Of those specialists who work in the private sector, 13 percent work in administrative and support services; 10 percent work in professional, scientific, and technical services; 9 percent in finance and insurance firms; 9 percent in health care; and 7 percent in manufacturing. The companies that are most likely to hire personnel specialists are the larger ones, which have more employees to manage.

STARTING OUT

Colleges and universities have placement counselors who can help graduates find employment. In addition, large companies often send recruiters to campuses looking for promising job applicants. Otherwise, interested individuals may apply directly to local companies.

While still in high school, you may apply for entry-level jobs as personnel clerks and assistants. Private employment agencies and local offices of the state employment service are other possible sources for work. In addition, newspaper want ads often contain listings of many personnel jobs.

Beginners in personnel work are trained on the job or in formal training programs, where they learn how to classify jobs, interview applicants, or administer employee benefits. Then they are assigned to specialized areas in the personnel department. Some people enter the labor relations field after first gaining experience in general personnel work, but it is becoming more common for qualified individuals to enter that field directly.

ADVANCEMENT

After trainees have mastered basic personnel tasks, they are assigned to specific areas in the department to gain specialized experience. In time, they may advance to supervisory positions or to manager of a major part of the personnel program, such as training, compensation, or EEO/affirmative action. Advancement may also be achieved by moving into a higher position in a smaller organization. A few experienced employees with exceptional ability ultimately become top executives with titles such as director of personnel or director of labor relations. As in most fields, employees with advanced education and a proven record of accomplishment are the most likely to advance in human resources positions.

EARNINGS

Jobs for personnel and labor relations specialists pay salaries that vary widely depending on the nature of the business and the size and location of the firm, as well as on the individual's qualifications and experience.

According to a survey conducted by the National Association of Colleges and Employers, an entry-level human resources specialist with a bachelor's degree in human resources, including labor and industrial relations, earned $41,680 annually in 2007.

The U.S. Department of Labor (USDL) reports that median annual earnings of human resources, training, and labor relations specialists were $52,270 in 2006. Salaries ranged from less than $26,000 to more than $88,630. The USDL reports the following mean salaries for human resources professionals by industry: federal government, $72,240; local government, $52,960; employment services, $47,760; and business, professional, labor, political, and similar organizations, $46,260. Human resources managers earned salaries that ranged from less than $51,810 to $114,860 or more in 2006.

WORK ENVIRONMENT

Personnel employees work under pleasant conditions in modern offices. Personnel specialists are seldom required to work more than 35 or 40 hours per week, although they may do so if they are developing a program or special project. The specific hours you work as a personnel specialist may depend upon which company employs you. "I work Monday through Friday," says Susan Eckerle, "but if you work for a company that has weekend hours, you'll probably have to work some weekends too. If you never work weekends, you won't know your employees."

Labor relations specialists often work longer hours, especially when contract agreements are being prepared and negotiated. The difficult aspects of the work may involve firing people, taking disciplinary actions, or handling employee disputes.

OUTLOOK

The U.S. Department of Labor (USDL) predicts that there will be faster-than-average growth through 2016 for human resources, training, and labor relations managers and specialists. The USDL predicts especially strong growth for training and development specialists and employment, recruitment, and placement specialists.

Competition for jobs will continue to be strong, however, as there will be an abundance of qualified applicants. Opportunities will be best in the private sector as businesses continue to increase their staffs as they begin to devote more resources to increasing employee productivity, retraining, safety, and benefits. Employment should also be strong with consulting firms that offer personnel and benefits and compensation services to businesses that cannot afford to have their own extensive staffs. As jobs change with new technology, more employers will need training specialists to teach new skills. Personnel specialist jobs may be affected by the trend in corporate downsizing and restructuring. Applicants who are certified will have the best prospects for employment.

FOR MORE INFORMATION

For information on standards and procedures in arbitration, contact
American Arbitration Association
1633 Broadway, 10th Floor
New York, NY 10019-6705
Tel: 212-716-5800
http://www.adr.org

For information on certification, contact
American Society for Training and Development
1640 King Street, Box 1443
Alexandria, VA 22313-2043
Tel: 703-683-8100
http://www.astd.org

For information about certification, contact
International Foundation of Employee Benefits Plans
PO Box 69
Brookfield, WI 53008-0069
Tel: 888-334-3327
http://www.ifebp.org

For information on training, job opportunities, and human resources publications, contact
International Public Management Association for Human Resources
1617 Duke Street
Alexandria, VA 22314-3406
Tel: 703-549-7100
http://www.ipma-hr.org

For general information on labor relations, contact
Labor and Employment Relations Association
University of Illinois—Urbana-Champaign
121 Labor and Industrial Relations Building
504 East Armory
Champaign, IL 61820-6221
Tel: 217-333-0072
Email: LERAoffice@uiuc.edu
http://www.lera.uiuc.edu

For information on certification and to use an interactive career mapping tool, visit the society's Web site:
Society for Human Resource Management
1800 Duke Street
Alexandria, VA 22314-3494
Tel: 800-283-7476
http://www.shrm.org

For news and information on compensation and benefits administration and certification, contact
WorldatWork
14040 North Northsight Boulevard
Scottsdale, AZ 85260-3601
Tel: 877-951-9191
http://www.worldatwork.org

Property and Real Estate Managers

OVERVIEW

Property and real estate managers plan and supervise the activities that affect land and buildings. Most of them manage rental properties, such as apartment buildings, office buildings, and shopping centers. Others manage the services and commonly owned areas of condominiums and community associations. Approximately 329,000 property and real estate managers are employed in the United States.

HISTORY

The first property managers, in the early 1900s, were real estate agents who earned additional income by collecting rent and negotiating leases. During the 1920s, the job became a menial position that was necessary in a real estate brokerage firm but was not considered a full-fledged part of the business. After the collapse of the financial market in 1929, banks, insurance companies, and other mortgage holders found themselves owners of multiple properties because of foreclosures. These new owners had neither the skills nor the inclination to manage the properties. Suddenly, the position of "rent man," which had been despised in the 1920s, became more respected and more in demand.

The new importance of the property manager, plus a corresponding increase in industry abuses, led to the formation of a professional association for property managers, the Institute of Real Estate Management. The new members quickly set out to establish industry ethics

QUICK FACTS

School Subjects
Business
English
Mathematics

Personal Skills
Communication/ideas
Leadership/management

Work Environment
Primarily indoors
Primarily multiple locations

Minimum Education Level
Bachelor's degree

Salary Range
$20,140 to $43,070 to
$95,170+

Certification or Licensing
Voluntary (certification)
Required for certain
  positions (licensing)

Outlook
Faster than the average

DOT
186

GOE
13.01.01

NOC
0121

O*NET-SOC
11-9141.00

and standards, professional designations, and industry education and seminars.

THE JOB

Most property and real estate managers are responsible for day-to-day management of residential and commercial real estate and usually manage several properties at one time. Acting as the owners' agents and advisers, they supervise the marketing of space, negotiate lease agreements, direct bookkeeping activities, and report to owners on the status of the property. They also negotiate contracts for trash removal and other services and hire the maintenance and on-site management personnel employed at the properties.

Some managers buy and develop real estate for companies that have widespread retail operations, such as franchise restaurants and hotel chains, or for companies that build such projects as shopping malls and industrial parks.

On-site managers are based at the properties they manage and may even live on the property. Most of them are responsible for apartment buildings and work under the direction of property managers. They train, supervise, and assign duties to maintenance staffs; inspect the properties to determine what maintenance and repairs are needed; schedule routine service of heating and air-conditioning systems; keep records of operating costs; and submit cost reports to the property managers or owners. They deal with residents on a daily basis and are responsible for handling their requests for service and repairs, resolving complaints concerning other tenants, and enforcing rules and lease restrictions.

Apartment house managers work for property owners or property management firms and are usually on-site managers. They show apartments to prospective tenants, negotiate leases, collect rents, handle tenants' requests, and direct the activities of maintenance staffs and outside contractors.

Building superintendents are responsible for operating and maintaining the facilities and equipment of such properties as apartment houses and office buildings. At small properties, the superintendent may be the only on-site manager and report directly to property managers; at larger properties, superintendents may report to on-site managers and supervise maintenance staffs.

Housing project managers direct the operation of housing projects provided for such groups as military families, low-income families, and welfare recipients. The housing is usually subsidized by the government and may consist of single-family homes, multiunit dwellings, or house trailers.

Condominium managers are responsible to unit-owner associations and manage the services and commonly owned areas of condominium properties. They submit reports to the association members, supervise collection of owner assessments, resolve owners' complaints, and direct the activities of maintenance staffs and outside contractors. In some communities, such as planned unit developments, homeowners belong to associations that employ managers to oversee the homeowners' jointly used properties and facilities.

Real estate asset managers work for institutional owners such as banks and insurance companies. Their responsibilities are larger in scope. Rather than manage day-to-day property operations, asset managers usually have an advisory role regarding the acquisition, rehabilitation, refinancing, and disposition of properties in a particular portfolio, and they may act for the owner in making specific business decisions, such as selecting and supervising site managers, authorizing operating expenditures, reviewing and approving leases, and monitoring local market conditions.

Specialized property and real estate managers perform a variety of other types of functions. *Market managers* direct the activities of municipal, regional, or state markets where wholesale fruit, vegetables, or meat are sold. They rent space to buyers and sellers and direct the supervisors who are responsible for collecting fees, maintaining and cleaning the buildings and grounds, and enforcing sanitation and security rules. *Public events facilities rental managers* negotiate contracts with organizations that wish to lease arenas, auditoriums, stadiums, or other facilities that are used for public events. They solicit new business and renewals of established contracts, maintain schedules to determine the availability of the facilities for bookings, and oversee operation and maintenance activities.

Real estate firm managers direct the activities of the *sales agents* who work for real estate firms. They screen and hire sales agents and conduct training sessions. They confer with agents and clients to resolve such problems as adjusting selling prices and determining who is responsible for repairs and closing costs. *Business opportunity-and-property-investment brokers* buy and sell business enterprises and investment properties on a commission or speculative basis. They investigate such factors as the financial ratings of businesses that are for sale, the desirability of a property's location for various types of businesses, and the condition of investment properties.

Businesses employ real estate managers to find, acquire, and develop the properties they need for their operations and to dispose of properties they no longer need. Real estate agents often work for companies that operate retail merchandising chains, such as fast food restaurants, gasoline stations, and apparel shops. They locate sites that are desirable for their companies' operations and arrange to purchase or lease them. They also review their companies' holdings to identify properties that are no longer desirable and then negotiate to dispose of them. (*Real estate sales agents* also may be called real estate agents, but they are not involved in property management.) *Land development managers* are responsible for acquiring land for such projects as shopping centers and industrial parks. They negotiate with local governments, property owners, and public interest groups to eliminate obstacles to their companies' developments, and they arrange for architects to draw up plans and construction firms to build the projects.

REQUIREMENTS

High School
High school students interested in this field should enroll in college preparatory programs that include classes in business, mathematics, speech, and English.

Postsecondary Training
Most employers prefer college graduates for property and real estate management positions. They prefer degrees in real estate, business management, finance, and related fields, but they also consider liberal arts graduates. In some cases, inexperienced college graduates with bachelor's or master's degrees enter the field as assistant property managers.

Many property and real estate managers attend training programs offered by various professional and trade associations. Employers often send their managers to these programs to improve their management skills and expand their knowledge of such subjects as operation and maintenance of building mechanical systems, insurance and risk management, business and real estate law, and accounting and financial concepts. Many managers attend these programs voluntarily to prepare for advancement to positions with more responsibility.

Certification or Licensing
Certification or licensing is not required for most property managers. Managers who have appropriate experience, complete required training programs, and achieve satisfactory scores on written exams, however, can earn certification and such professional designations as certified property manager and accredited residential manager (which are offered by the Institute of Real Estate Management) and

real property administrator and facilities management administrator (which are offered by BOMI International). Such designations are usually looked upon favorably by employers as a sign of a person's competence and dedication. Other organizations that offer certification include the Community Associations Institute and the National Board of Certification for Community Association Managers.

The federal government requires certification for managers of public housing that is subsidized by federal funds. Business opportunity-and-property-investment brokers must hold state licenses, and some states require real estate managers to hold licenses.

Other Requirements

Property and real estate managers must be skilled in both oral and written communications and be adept at dealing with people. They need to be good administrators and negotiators, and those who specialize in land development must be especially resourceful and creative to arrange financing for their projects. Managers for small rental or condominium complexes may be required to have building repair and maintenance skills as well as business management skills.

EXPLORING

If you are interested in property and real estate management, participate in activities that help you develop management skills, such as serving as an officer in an organization or participating in Junior Achievement (http://www.ja.org) projects. Part-time or summer jobs in sales or volunteer work that involves contact with the public would be good experience.

You may be able to tour apartment complexes, shopping centers, and other real estate developments and should take advantage of any opportunities to talk with property and real estate managers about their careers.

EMPLOYERS

Approximately 329,000 people in the United States are employed as property and real estate managers. About 36 percent work for real estate agents and brokers, lessors of real estate, or property management firms. Others work for real estate developers, government agencies that manage public buildings, corporations with large property holdings used for their retail operations, real estate investors, and mining and oil companies. Many are self-employed as developers, apartment building owners, property management firm owners, or owners of full-service real estate businesses. More than 50 percent of all property and real estate managers are self-employed.

STARTING OUT

Students who are about to graduate from college can obtain assistance from their career services offices in finding their first job. You can also apply directly to property management firms and check ads in the help wanted sections of local newspapers. Property and real estate managers often begin as on-site managers for small apartment house complexes, condominiums, or community associations. Some property managers begin as real estate agents or in another position in a real estate firm and later move into property management.

ADVANCEMENT

With experience, entry-level property and site managers may transfer to larger properties or they may become assistant property managers, working closely with property managers and acquiring experience in a variety of management tasks. Assistant managers may advance to property manager positions, in which they most likely will be responsible for several properties. As they advance in their careers, property managers may manage larger or more complex operations, specialize in managing specific types of property, or possibly establish their own companies.

To be considered for advancement, property managers must demonstrate the ability to deal effectively with tenants, contractors, and maintenance staff. They must be capable administrators and possess business skills, initiative, good organization, and excellent communication skills.

EARNINGS

Managers of residential and commercial rental real estate are usually compensated by a fee based on the gross rental income of the properties. Managers of condominiums and other homeowner-occupied properties also are usually paid on a fee basis. Site managers and others employed by a management company are typically salaried.

According to the U.S. Department of Labor, annual earnings for all property managers in 2006 ranged from less than $20,140 to $95,170 or more. The median annual salary for property managers in 2006 was $43,070.

Property and real estate managers usually receive such benefits as medical and health insurance. On-site apartment building managers may have rent-free apartments, and many managers have the use of company automobiles. In addition, managers involved in land development may receive a small percentage of ownership in their projects.

WORK ENVIRONMENT

Property and real estate managers usually work in offices but may spend much of their time at the properties they manage. On-site apartment building managers often leave their offices to inspect other areas, check maintenance or repair work, or resolve problems reported by tenants.

Many apartment managers must live in the buildings they manage so they can be available in emergencies, and they may be required to show apartments to prospective tenants at night or on weekends. Property and real estate managers may attend evening meetings with property owners, association boards of directors, or civic groups interested in property planned for development. Real estate managers who work for large companies frequently travel to inspect their companies' property holdings or locate properties their companies might acquire.

OUTLOOK

Employment of property and real estate managers is expected to increase faster than the average for all occupations through 2016, according to the U.S. Department of Labor. Job openings are expected to occur as older, experienced managers transfer to other occupations or leave the labor force. The best opportunities will be for college graduates with degrees in real estate, business administration, and related fields and who also possess professional certifications.

In the next decade, many of the economy's new jobs are expected to be in wholesale and retail trade, finance, insurance, real estate, and other service industries. Growth in these industries will bring a need for more office and retail properties and for people to manage them.

In housing, there will be a greater demand for apartments because of the high cost of owning a home. New home developments also are increasingly organized with community or homeowner associations that require managers. In addition, more owners of commercial and multiunit residential properties are expected to use professional managers to help make their properties more profitable. The growing number of people age 65 and over will create a need for the construction of assisted-living and retirement communities, and managers will be needed to oversee these facilities.

FOR MORE INFORMATION

For information on certification, contact
BOMI International
One Park Place, Suite 475
Annapolis, MD 21401-3479
Tel: 800-235-2664
Email: service@bomi.org
http://www.bomi-edu.org

For information on educational programs, contact
Building Owners and Managers Association International
1101 15th Street, NW, Suite 800
Washington, DC 20005-5021
Tel: 202-408-2662
Email: info@boma.org
http://www.boma.org

For information on certification, contact
Community Associations Institute
225 Reinekers Lane, Suite 300
Alexandria, VA 22314-2875
Tel: 888-224-4321
http://www.caionline.org

For information on training programs, certification, and industry research, contact
Institute of Real Estate Management
430 North Michigan Avenue
Chicago, IL 60611-4011
Tel: 800-837-0706
Email: custserv@irem.org
http://www.irem.org

This organization is devoted to the multifamily housing industry and represents developers, owners, managers, and suppliers.
National Apartment Association
4300 Wilson Boulevard, Suite 400
Arlington, VA 22203-4168
Tel: 703-518-6141
http://www.naahq.org

For information on certification, contact
National Board of Certification for Community Association Managers
225 Reinekers Lane, Suite 310
Alexandria, VA 22314-2856
Tel: 703-836-6902
Email: info@nbccam.org
http://www.nbccam.org

For information on property management in Canada, contact
Canadian Real Estate Association
200 Catherine Street, 6th Floor
Ottawa, ON K2P 2K9 Canada
Tel: 613-237-7111
Email: info@crea.ca
http://crea.ca

Restaurant and Food Service Managers

QUICK FACTS

School Subjects
Business
Mathematics

Personal Skills
Communication/ideas
Leadership/management

Work Environment
Primarily indoors
Primarily one location

Minimum Education Level
High school diploma

Salary Range
$27,000 to $43,020 to
$100,000+

Certification or Licensing
Voluntary

Outlook
More slowly than the average

DOT
157

GOE
11.01.01

NOC
0631

O*NET-SOC
11-9051.00, 35-1012.00

OVERVIEW

Restaurant and food service managers are responsible for the overall operation of businesses that serve food. Food service work includes the purchasing of a variety of food, selection of the menu, preparation of the food, and, most importantly, maintenance of health and sanitation levels. It is the responsibility of managers to oversee staffing for each task in addition to performing the business and accounting functions of restaurant operations. There are approximately 350,000 food service managers employed in the United States.

HISTORY

The word *restaurant* comes from the French word *restaurer,* meaning "to restore." It is believed that the term was first used in its present sense in the 18th century by a soup vendor in Paris, who offered his customers a choice of soups, or *restoratives* (restaurants). The first restaurants in the United States were patterned after European restaurants and coffeehouses. During the 20th century, many innovations in the restaurant industry led to the development of new kinds of eating establishments, including the cafeteria, Automat, counter-service restaurant, drive-in, and fast food chain.

THE JOB

Restaurant and food service managers work in restaurants ranging from elegant hotel dining rooms to fast food restaurants. They also may work in food service facilities ranging from school cafeterias to hospital food services. Whatever the setting, these managers coordinate and direct the work of the employees who prepare and serve food and perform other related functions. Restaurant managers set work schedules for wait staff and host staff. Food service managers are responsible for buying the food and equipment necessary for the operation of the restaurant or facility, and they may help with menu planning. They inspect the premises periodically to ensure compliance with health and sanitation regulations. Restaurant and food service managers perform many clerical and financial duties, such as keeping records, directing payroll operations, handling large sums of money, and taking inventories. Their work usually involves much contact with customers and vendors, such as taking suggestions, handling complaints, and creating a friendly atmosphere. Restaurant managers generally supervise any advertising or sales promotions for their operations.

In some very large restaurants and institutional food service facilities, one or more *assistant managers* and an *executive chef* or *food manager* assist the manager. These specially trained assistants oversee service in the dining room and other areas of the operation and supervise the kitchen staff and preparation of all foods served.

Restaurant and food service managers are responsible for the success of their establishments. They continually analyze every aspect of its operation and make whatever changes are needed to guarantee its profitability.

These duties are common, in varying degrees, to both *owner-managers* of relatively small restaurants and to nonowner-managers who may be salaried employees in large restaurants or institutional food service facilities. The owner-manager of a restaurant is more likely to be involved in service functions, sometimes operating the cash register, waiting on tables, and performing a wide variety of tasks.

REQUIREMENTS
Educational requirements for restaurant and food service managers vary greatly. In many cases, no specific requirements exist and managerial positions are filled by promoting experienced food and beverage preparation and service workers. However, as more colleges offer programs in restaurant and institutional food service management—programs that combine academic work with on-the-job experience—more restaurant and food service chains are seeking individuals with this training.

Postsecondary Training
Many colleges and universities offer four-year programs leading to a bachelor's degree in restaurant and hotel management or

institutional food service management. Some individuals qualify for management training by earning an associate's degree or other formal award below the bachelor's degree level from one of the nearly 1,000 community and junior colleges, technical institutes, or other institutions that offer programs in these fields. Students hired as management trainees by restaurant chains and food service management companies undergo vigorous training programs.

The U.S. Department of Labor reports that more than 40 percent of restaurant and food service managers have a high school diploma or less and only less than 25 percent have a bachelor's or graduate degree. Those interested in working at higher-end restaurants, chains, or opening their own restaurant should earn at least a bachelor's degree in restaurant management or a related field.

Certification or Licensing

The National Restaurant Association Educational Foundation offers a voluntary foodservice management professional certification to restaurant and food service managers. The International Food Service Executives Association also offers several voluntary certification designations. Contact the associations for more information.

Other Requirements

Experience in all areas of restaurant and food service work is an important requirement for successful managers. Managers must be familiar with the various operations of the establishment: food preparation, service operations, sanitary regulations, and financial functions.

One of the most important requirements for restaurant and food service managers is to have good business knowledge. They must possess a high degree of technical knowledge in handling business details, such as buying large items of machinery and equipment and large quantities of food. Desirable personality characteristics include poise, self-confidence, and an ability to get along with people. Managers may be on their feet for long periods, and the hours of work may be both long and irregular.

EXPLORING

Practical restaurant and food service experience is usually easy to get. In colleges with curriculum offerings in these areas, summer jobs in all phases of the work are available and, in some cases, required. Some restaurant and food service chains provide on-the-job training in management.

A manager *(center)* and his staff examine fruit in a restaurant kitchen. Only the best-quality fruit will be served to customers. *(Jim West Photography)*

EMPLOYERS

Approximately 350,000 food service managers are employed in the United States. Restaurants and food service make up one of the largest and most active sectors of the nation's economy. Employers include restaurants of various sizes, hotel dining rooms, ships, trains, institutional food service facilities, and many other establishments where food is served. No matter the size or style of the establishment, managers are needed to oversee the operation and to ensure that records are kept, goals are met, and things run smoothly. About 45 percent of restaurant and food service managers are self-employed. They own independent restaurants or other small food service establishments.

STARTING OUT

Many restaurants and food service facilities provide self-sponsored, on-the-job training for prospective managers. There are still cases in which people work hard and move up the ladder within the organization's workforce, finally arriving at the managerial position. More and more, people with advanced education and specialized training move directly into manager-trainee positions and then on to managerial positions.

ADVANCEMENT

In large restaurants and food service organizations, promotion opportunities frequently arise for employees with knowledge of the overall operation. Experience in all aspects of the work is an important consideration for the food service employee who desires advancement. The employee with knowledge of kitchen operations may advance from pantry supervisor to food manager, assistant manager, and finally restaurant or food service manager. Similar advancement is possible for dining room workers with knowledge of kitchen operations.

Advancement to top executive positions is possible for managers employed by large restaurant and institutional food service chains. A good educational background and some specialized training are increasingly valuable assets to employees who hope to advance.

EARNINGS

The earnings of salaried restaurant and food service managers vary a great deal, depending on the type and size of the establishment. According to the U.S. Department of Labor, median annual earnings of food service managers were $43,020 in 2006. The lowest paid 10 percent earned less than $27,400, and the highest paid 10 percent earned more than $70,810. Those in charge of the largest restaurants and institutional food service facilities often earn more than $100,000. Managers of fast food restaurants average about $27,000 per year. In addition to a base salary, most managers receive bonuses based on profits, which can range from $2,000 to $7,500 a year.

WORK ENVIRONMENT

Work environments are usually pleasant. There is usually a great deal of activity involved in preparing and serving food to large numbers of people, and managers usually work 40 to 48 hours per week. In some cafeterias, especially those located within an industry or business establishment, hours are regular, and little evening work is required. Many restaurants serve late dinners, however, necessitating the manager to remain on duty during a late-evening work period.

Many restaurants furnish meals to employees during their work hours. Annual bonuses, group plan pensions, hospitalization, medical, and other benefits may be offered to restaurant managers.

OUTLOOK

Employment for restaurant and food service managers will grow more slowly than the average for all occupations through 2016. Those with bachelor's or associate's degrees will have stronger employment opportunities.

Despite the prediction for slow growth, there should continue to be opportunities in the field. New restaurants are always opening to meet increasing demand. It has been estimated that at least 44 percent of all of the food consumed in the United States is eaten in restaurants and hotels. Many job openings will arise from the need to replace managers retiring from the workforce. Also, population growth will result in an increased demand for full-service restaurants and, in turn, a need for managers to oversee them. As the elderly population increases, managers will be needed to staff dining rooms located in hospitals and nursing homes. Opportunities will also be good for managers in special food services such as schools, healthcare facilities, hotels, and other businesses that contract out their food service needs (especially nursing and residential care facilities).

Economic downswings have a great effect on eating and drinking establishments. During a recession, people have less money to spend on luxuries such as dining out, thus hurting the restaurant business. However, greater numbers of working parents and their families are finding it convenient to eat out or purchase carryout food from a restaurant.

FOR MORE INFORMATION

For information on restaurant management careers, education, and certification, contact the following organizations:

International Council on Hotel, Restaurant and Institutional Education
2810 North Parham, Suite 230
Richmond, VA 23294-4422
Tel: 804-346-4800
Email: info@chrie.org
http://chrie.org

International Food Service Executives Association
2609 Surfwood Drive
Las Vegas, NV 89128-7183
Tel: 800-893-5499
Email: hq@ifsea.com
http://www.ifsea.com

National Restaurant Association Educational Foundation
175 West Jackson Boulevard, Suite 1500
Chicago, IL 60604-2814
Tel: 800-765-2122
Email: info@restaurant.org
http://www.nraef.org

Canadian Restaurant and Foodservices Association
316 Bloor Street West
Toronto, ON M5S 1W5 Canada
Tel: 800-387-5649
Email: info@crfa.ca
http://www.crfa.ca

Retail Business Owners

OVERVIEW

Retail business owners are entrepreneurs who start or buy their own businesses or franchise operations. They are responsible for all aspects of a business operation, from planning and ordering merchandise to overseeing day-to-day operations. Retail business owners sell such items as clothing, household appliances, groceries, jewelry, and furniture.

HISTORY

Retailing is a vital commercial activity, providing customers with an opportunity to purchase goods and services from various types of merchants. The first retail outlets in America were trading posts and general stores. At trading posts, goods obtained from Native Americans were exchanged for items imported from Europe or manufactured in other parts of the country. As villages and towns grew, trading posts developed into general stores and began to sell food, farm necessities, and clothing. Typically run by a single person, these stores sometimes served as the post office and became the social and economic center of their communities.

Since World War II, giant supermarkets, discount houses, chain stores, and shopping malls have grown in popularity. Even so, individually owned businesses still thrive, often giving customers more personal and better-informed service. Moreover, despite the large growth in retail outlets and the increased competition that has accompanied it, retailing still provides the same basic, important function it did in the early years of the United States.

THE JOB

Although retail business owners sell a wide variety of products, from apples to automobiles, the basic job responsibilities remain the same. Simply stated, the retail business owner must do everything necessary to ensure the successful operation of a business.

There are five major categories of job responsibilities within a retail establishment: merchandising and buying, store operations, sales promotion and advertising, bookkeeping and accounting, and personnel supervision. Merchandising and buying determine the type and amount of actual goods to be sold. Store operations involve maintaining the building and providing for the movement of goods and personnel within the building. Sales promotion and advertising are the marketing methods used to inform customers and potential customers about the goods and services that are available. In bookkeeping and accounting, records are kept of payroll, taxes, and money spent and received. Personnel involves staffing the store with people who are trained and qualified to handle all the work that needs to be done.

The owner must be aware of all aspects of the business operation so that he or she can make informed decisions. Specific duties of an individual owner depend on the size of the store and the number of employees. In a store with more than 10 employees, many of the operational, promotional, and personnel activities may be supervised by a manager. The owner may plan the overall purpose and function of the store and hire a manager to oversee the day-to-day operations. In a smaller store, the owner may also do much of the operational activities, including sweeping the floor, greeting customers, and balancing the accounting books.

In both large and small operations, an owner must keep up to date on product information, as well as on economic and technological conditions that may have an impact on business. This entails reading catalogs about product availability, checking current inventories and prices, and researching and implementing any technological advances that may make the operation more efficient. For example, an owner may decide to purchase data processing equipment to help with accounting functions, as well as to generate a mailing list to inform customers of special sales.

Because of the risks involved in opening a business and the many economic and managerial demands put on individual owners, a desire to open a retail business should be combined with proper management skills, sufficient economic backing, and a good sense of what the public wants. The large majority of retail businesses fail because of a lack of managerial experience on the part of owners.

Franchise ownership, whereby an individual owner obtains a license to sell an existing company's goods or services, grew phenomenally during the 1980s. Franchise agreements enable the person who wants to open a business to receive expert advice from the sponsoring company about location, hiring and training of employees, arrangement of merchandise, display of goods, and record keeping. Some entrepreneurs, however, do not want to be limited to the product lines and other restrictions that accompany running a franchise store. Franchise operations also may fail, but their likelihood of success is greater than that of a totally independent retail store.

REQUIREMENTS
High School
A high school diploma is important in order to understand the basics of business ownership, though there are no specific educational or experiential requirements for this position. Course work in business administration is helpful, as is previous experience in the retail trade. Hard work, constant analysis and evaluation, and sufficient capital are important elements of a successful business venture.

If you are interested in owning a business, you should take courses in mathematics, business management, and in business-related subjects, such as accounting, typing, and computer science. In addition, pursue English and other courses that enhance your communications skills. Specific skill areas also should be developed. For example, if you want to open an electronics repair shop, you should learn as much about electronics as possible.

Owners of small retail businesses often manage the store and work behind the counter. In such a case, the owner of a meat market is the butcher as well.

Postsecondary Training
As the business environment gets more and more competitive, many people are opting for an academic degree as a way of getting more training. A bachelor's program emphasizing business communications, marketing, business law, business management, and accounting should be pursued. Some people choose to get a master's in business administration or other related graduate degree. There are also special business schools that offer a one- or two-year program in business management. Some correspondence schools also offer courses on how to plan and run a business.

The owners of a bakery wait on a customer. *(Jim West Photography)*

Certification or Licensing

A business license may be a requirement in some states. Individual states or communities may have zoning codes or other regulations specifying what type of business can be located in a particular area. Check with your state's chamber of commerce or department of revenue for more information on obtaining a license, or visit this Web site: http://www.sba.gov/hotlist/license.html.

Other Requirements

Whatever the experience and training, a retail business owner needs a lot of energy, patience, and fortitude to overcome the slow times and other difficulties involved in running a business. Other important personal characteristics include maturity, creativity, and good business judgment. Retail business owners also should be able to motivate employees and delegate authority.

EXPLORING

Working full or part time as a sales clerk or in some other capacity within a retail business is a good way to learn about the responsibilities of operating a business. Talking with owners of small shops is also helpful, as is reading periodicals that publish articles on self-employment, such as *Entrepreneur* magazine (http://www. entrepreneur.com).

Most communities have a chamber of commerce whose members usually will be glad to share their insights into the career of a retail business owner. The Small Business Administration, an agency of the U.S. government, is another possible source of information.

EMPLOYERS

Retail is the second-largest industry in the United States, employing more than 24 million Americans and generating more than $4.7 trillion in retail sales annually, according to the National Retail Federation. Over 95 percent of all U.S. retailers are single-store businesses, but they generate less than 50 percent of all retail store sales, according to About.com: Retail Industry.

STARTING OUT

Few people start their career as an owner. Many start as a manager or in some other position within a retail business. While developing managerial skills or while pursuing a college degree or other relevant training, you should decide what type of business you would like to own. Many people decide to buy an existing business because it already has a proven track record and because banks and other lending institutions often are more likely to loan money to an existing facility. A retail business owner should anticipate having at least 50 percent of the money needed to start or buy a business. Some people find it helpful to have one or more partners in a business venture.

Owning a franchise is another way of starting a business without a large capital investment, as franchise agreements often involve some assistance in planning and start-up costs. Franchise operations, however, are not necessarily less expensive to run than a totally independent business.

ADVANCEMENT

Because an owner is by definition the boss, there are limited opportunities for advancement. Advancement often takes the form of expansion of an existing business, leading to increased earnings and prestige. Expanding a business also can entail added risk, as it involves increasing operational costs. A successful franchise owner may be offered an additional franchise location or an executive position at the corporate headquarters.

A small number of successful independent business owners choose to franchise their business operations in different areas. Some owners become part-time consultants, while others teach a course at a college or university or in an adult education program. This teaching often is done not only for the financial rewards but also as a way of helping others investigate the option of retail ownership.

EARNINGS

Earnings vary widely and are greatly influenced by the ability of the individual owner, the type of product or service being sold, and existing economic conditions. Some retail business owners may earn less than $15,000 a year, while the most successful owners earn $100,000 or more.

WORK ENVIRONMENT

Retail business owners generally work in pleasant surroundings. Even so, ownership is a demanding occupation, with owners often working six or seven days a week. Working more than 60 hours a week is not unusual, especially during the Christmas season and other busy times. An owner of a large establishment may be able to leave a manager in charge of many parts of the business, but the owner still must be available to solve any pressing concerns. Owners of small businesses often stay in the store throughout the day, spending much of the time on their feet.

A retail business owner may occasionally travel out of town to attend conferences or to solicit new customers and product information. An owner of a small business, especially, should develop a close relationship with steady customers.

OUTLOOK

The retail field is extremely competitive, and many businesses fail each year. The most common reason for failure is poor management. Thus, people with some managerial experience or training will likely have the best chance at running a successful business.

Increasing unemployment, the weakening of consumer confidence, increased competition from other retailers and direct-marketers, and the growth of Internet businesses are just some of the issues retail businesses will face in the next decade.

FOR MORE INFORMATION

The following foundation conducts research and analysis of women-owned businesses
Center for Women's Business Research
1411 K Street, NW, Suite 1350
Washington, DC 20005-3407
Tel: 202-638-3060
Email: info@womensbusinessresearch.org
http://www.nfwbo.org

For materials on educational programs in the retail industry, contact
National Retail Federation
325 7th Street, NW, Suite 1100
Washington, DC 20004-2818
Tel: 800-673-4692
http://www.nrf.com

For information on jobs in retail, contact
Retail Industry Leaders Association
1700 North Moore Street, Suite 2250
Arlington, VA 22209-1933
Tel: 703-841-2300
http://www.retail-leaders.org

For a business starter packet with information about their loan program and services, and basic facts about starting a business, contact
U.S. Small Business Administration
409 Third Street, SW
Washington, DC 20416-0001
Tel: 800-827-5722
Email: answerdesk@sba.gov
http://www.sbaonline.sba.gov

INTERVIEW

James Regan is the owner/president of Big Picture Framing in South Burlington, Vermont. He discussed his career with the editors of Careers in Focus: Business Managers.

Q. Please tell us a little about yourself and your business.
A. I graduated from Boys Town High School in Nebraska and continued on to receive my B.A. from Saint Michael's College in

Colchester, Vermont. After graduation, I worked in the blue-collar world for four to five years before advancing to the "corporate" world, where I worked for an engineering firm for 12 years in Vermont. Once I got to the level of senior project manager, I saw there was nowhere else to go besides becoming an owner and that probably would've taken another 10 years. The company gave us quite a bit of autonomy and this eventually gave me a greater desire to be on my own. This desire and not being able to reach my financial and personal free-time goals led me to decide to go into business for myself. So, I left the company and traveled to South America and Spain. This gave me the much needed time away from the business world to figure out what I really wanted to do, what I was really passionate about. I had always wanted to get back into my short story writing so I looked for something that would work with that side of the brain and hopefully not be as stressful as the corporate world. My passion for the arts led me to a franchise in custom picture framing after generating a very in-depth business plan. The goal is to write in the morning and open the store at 10 a.m., and that's where I'm at now.

Q. What do you like most and least about your job?

A. I like seeing different art and meeting new people in a no-pressure, casual environment everyday. The downside at present is that I'm still in that three-year startup phase, so the business is not as lucrative as I'd like it to be. But I'm much happier and enjoying life more so than when I was in the corporate world working for someone else. We're growing everyday and I always have hope . . . it just takes awhile to really become part of the community.

Q. What is your work environment like?

A. The work environment is very low-key, casual, and fun . . . people walk in the door with their dogs. Some days, when there are artists and customers in at the same time, the conversations are really great, ranging from art for arts sake to the many issues at large in the world today. The shop takes on the ambience of a cozy coffee shop where everyone is comfortable being themselves. The end result is the customer leaving with the feeling of time well spent and enjoyed as well as anticipating what their art is going to look like hanging on the wall.

Q. What advice would you give to high school students who are interested in becoming business owners?

A. Become involved in as many activities as possible: Getting to know how other people's minds work, how everyone is different—and that it's OK—is essential to any business owner. The interactions you have as a youth will wire your brain for how you deal with yourself, people, and situations in the future; if not wired right, it can be very hard to change or overcome the learned ways of the past when confronted with the many obstacles you are certainly bound to encounter in life as well as in the business world.

Q. What are the three most important professional qualities for business owners/managers?

A. Being honest, straightforward, and sympathetic is a good start to any business venture. The lack of any of these traits will come back to bite you eventually, especially if you're dealing with the general public. All it takes is for one person, whether right or wrong unfortunately, to adversely sway someone else's opinion and hence the beginning of a domino effect that may lead to the downfall of a business, especially in a small community.

The customer is always right. Yes, it is a cliché, but it's a good one. Bending over backwards for a customer will most likely not bankrupt you but the inverse can and most likely will be far more detrimental to your business—they told two people, who told two people, and so on.

Just take one day at a time doing the best you can. Stay in the NOW while working toward your goals. Quality and timeliness are essential. Most important though, I think, is having a real passion for what you do. If so, the rest will inherently fall into place. And lastly, don't let anybody tell you you can't do it—just look at all the Chinese restaurants in your neighborhood.

Retail Managers

QUICK FACTS

School Subjects
Business
Mathematics

Personal Skills
Helping/teaching
Leadership/management

Work Environment
Primarily indoors
Primarily one location

Minimum Education Level
High school diploma

Salary Range
$21,420 to $33,960 to
$100,000+

Certification or Licensing
None available

Outlook
More slowly than the average

DOT
185

GOE
10.01.01

NOC
0621, 6211

O*NET-SOC
41-1011.00

OVERVIEW

Retail managers are responsible for the profitable operation of retail trade establishments. They oversee the selling of food, clothing, furniture, sporting goods, novelties, and many other items. Their duties include hiring, training, and supervising other employees, maintaining the physical facilities, managing inventory, monitoring expenditures and receipts, and maintaining good public relations. Retail managers hold about 2.2 million jobs in the United States.

HISTORY

In the United States, small, family owned stores have been around for centuries. The first large chain store began to operate in the late 19th century. One of the aims of early chain stores was to provide staples for the pioneers of the newly settled West. Because chain store corporations were able to buy goods in large quantities and store them in warehouses, they were able to undersell private merchants.

The number of retail stores, especially supermarkets, began to grow rapidly during the 1930s. Stores often were owned and operated by chain corporations, which were able to benefit from bulk buying and more sophisticated storage practices. Cheaper transportation also contributed to the growth of retail stores because goods could be shipped and sold more economically.

Unlike the early family owned stores, giant retail outlets employed large numbers of people, requiring various levels of management to oversee the business. Retail managers were hired to oversee particular areas within department stores, for example, but higher level managers also were needed to make more general decisions about a company's goals and policies. Today, retailing is the second largest industry in the United States, employing more than 24 million people.

THE JOB

Retail managers are responsible for every phase of a store's operation. They often are one of the first employees to arrive in the morning and the last to leave at night. Their duties include hiring, training, and supervising other employees, maintaining the physical facilities, managing inventory, monitoring expenditures and receipts, and maintaining good public relations.

Perhaps the most important responsibility of retail managers is hiring and training qualified employees. Managers then assign duties to employees, monitor their progress, promote employees, and increase salaries when appropriate. When an employee's performance is not satisfactory, a manager must find a way to improve the performance or, if necessary, fire him or her.

Managers should be good at working with all different kinds of people. Differences of opinion and personality clashes among employees are inevitable, however, and the manager must be able to restore good feelings among the staff. Managers often have to deal with upset customers, and must attempt to restore goodwill toward the store when customers are dissatisfied.

Retail managers keep accurate and up-to-date records of store inventory. When new merchandise arrives, the manager ensures items are recorded, priced, and displayed or shelved. They must know when stock is getting low and order new items in a timely manner.

Some managers are responsible for merchandise promotions and advertising. The manager may confer with an advertising agency representative to determine appropriate advertising methods for the store. The manager also may decide what products to put on sale for advertising purposes.

The duties of store managers vary according to the type of merchandise sold, the size of the store, and the number of employees. In small, owner-operated stores, managers often are involved in accounting, data processing, marketing, research, sales, and shipping. In large retail corporations, however, managers may be involved in only one or two activities.

REQUIREMENTS

High School

You will need at least a high school education in order to become a retail manager. Helpful courses include business, mathematics,

The owner/manager *(right)* of a picture framing shop discusses a job with one of his employees. (Dennis MacDonald, Unicorn Stock Photos)

marketing, and economics. English and speech classes are also important. These courses will teach you to communicate effectively with all types of people, including employees and customers.

Postsecondary Training

Most retail stores prefer applicants with a college degree, and many hire only college graduates. Liberal arts, social sciences, and business are the most common degrees held by retail managers.

To prepare for a career as a retail store manager, take courses in accounting, business, marketing, English, advertising, and computer science. If you are unable to attend college as a full-time student, consider getting a job in a store to gain experience and attend college part time. All managers, regardless of their education, must have good marketing, analytical, communication, and people skills.

Many large retail stores and national chains have established formal training programs, including classroom instruction, for their new employees. The training period may last a week or as long as one year. Training for a department store manager, for example, may include working as a salesperson in several departments in order to learn about the store's operations.

Other Requirements

To be a successful retail manager, you should have good communication skills, enjoy working with and supervising people, and be willing to put in very long hours. Diplomacy often is necessary when creating schedules for workers and in disciplinary matters. There is a great deal of responsibility in retail management and such positions often are stressful. A calm disposition and ability to handle stress will serve you well.

EXPLORING

If you are interested in becoming a retail manager, you may be able to find part-time, weekend, or summer jobs in a clothing store, supermarket, or other retail trade establishment. You can gain valuable work experience through such jobs and will have the opportunity to observe the retail industry to determine whether you are interested in pursuing a career in it. It also is useful to read periodicals that publish articles on the retail field, such as *Stores* (http://www.stores. org), published by the National Retail Federation.

EMPLOYERS

There are about 2.2 million retail managers in the United States, and about 37 percent are self-employed (many are store owners). Nearly every type of retail business requires management, though small businesses may be run by their owners. Wherever retail sales

Mean Annual Earnings by Specialty, 2006

Software publishers	$86,030
Automobile dealers	$75,800
Building material and supplies dealers	$40,390
Clothing stores	$36,420
Grocery stores	$36,060
Gasoline stations	$31,390
Other general merchandise stores	$30,830

Source: U.S. Department of Labor

are made there is an opportunity for a management position, though most people have to begin in a much lower job. The food industry employs more workers than nearly any other business, and retail food businesses always need managers, though smaller businesses may not pay very well. In general, the larger the business and the bigger the city, the more a retail manager can earn. Most other retail managers work in grocery and department stores, motor vehicle dealerships, and clothing and accessory stores.

STARTING OUT

Many new college graduates are able to find managerial positions through their schools' career services office. Some of the large retail chains recruit on college campuses.

Not all store managers, however, are college graduates. Many store managers are promoted to their positions from jobs of less responsibility within their organization. Some may work in the retail industry for more than a dozen years before being promoted. Those with more education often receive promotions faster.

Regardless of educational background, people who are interested in the retail industry should consider working in a retail store at least part time or during the summer. Although there may not be an opening when the application is made, there often is a high turnover of employees in retail management, and vacancies occur frequently.

ADVANCEMENT

Advancement opportunities in retailing vary according to the size of the store, where the store is located, and the type of merchandise sold. Advancement also depends on the individual's work experience and educational background.

A store manager who works for a large retail chain, for example, may be given responsibility for a number of stores in a given area or region or transferred to a larger store in another city. Willingness to relocate to a new city may increase an employee's promotional opportunities.

Some managers decide to open their own stores after they have acquired enough experience in the retail industry. After working as a retail manager for a large chain of clothing stores, for example, a person may decide to open a small boutique.

Sometimes becoming a retail manager involves a series of promotions. A person who works in a supermarket, for example, may advance from clerk, checker, or bagger to a regular assignment in one of several departments in the store. After a period of time, he or she may become an assistant manager and eventually, a manager.

EARNINGS

Salaries depend on the size of the store, the responsibilities of the job, and the number of customers served. According to the U.S. Department of Labor, median annual earnings of supervisors of retail sales workers, including commission, were $33,960 in 2006. Salaries ranged from less than $21,420 to more than $59,710 per year. Mean annual earnings of grocery store managers were $36,060 in 2006, and managers of clothing stores earned $36,420. Those who managed other general merchandise stores earned $30,830, and those who managed building supply stores ranked among the highest paid at $40,390. Managers who oversee an entire region for a retail chain can earn more than $100,000.

In addition to a salary, some stores offer their managers special bonuses, or commissions, which are typically connected to the store's performance. Many stores also offer employee discounts on store merchandise.

WORK ENVIRONMENT

Most retail stores are pleasant places to work, and managers often are given comfortable offices. Many, however, work long hours. Managers often work six days a week and as many as 60 hours a week, especially during busy times of the year such as the Christmas season. Because holiday seasons are peak shopping periods, it is extremely rare that managers can take holidays off or schedule vacations around a holiday, even if the store is not open on that day.

Although managers usually can get away from the store during slow times, they must often be present if the store is open at night. It is important that the manager be available to handle the store's daily receipts, which usually are put in a safe or taken to a bank's night depository at the close of the business day.

OUTLOOK

Employment of retail managers is expected to grow more slowly than the average for all occupations through 2016, according to the U.S. Department of Labor. Although retailers have reduced their management staff to cut costs and make operations more efficient, there still are good opportunities in retailing. Internet stores and e-commerce ventures, for example, will present many new opportunities for retail managers. However, competition for all jobs will probably continue to increase, and computerized systems for inventory control may reduce the need for some managers. Applicants with the best educational backgrounds and work experience will have the best chances of finding jobs. There will always be a need for retail managers, however, as long as retail stores exist. Retail manager positions are rarely affected by corporate restructuring at retail headquarters; this has a greater impact on home office staff.

FOR MORE INFORMATION

For materials on educational programs in the retail industry, contact
National Retail Federation
325 7th Street, NW, Suite 1100
Washington, DC 20004-2818
Tel: 800-673-4692
http://www.nrf.com

For information on jobs in retail, contact
Retail Industry Leaders Association
1700 North Moore Street, Suite 2250
Arlington, VA 22209-1933
Tel: 703-841-2300
http://www.retail-leaders.org

Sports Executives

OVERVIEW

Sports executives, sometimes known as *team presidents*, *CEOs*, and *general managers*, manage professional, collegiate, and minor league sports teams. They are responsible for the teams' finances, as well as overseeing the other departments within the organization, such as marketing, public relations, accounting, ticket sales, advertising, sponsorship, and community relations. Sports executives also work on establishing long-term contacts and support within the communities where the teams play.

HISTORY

The sports industry has matured into one of the largest industries in the United States. Professional teams are the most widely recognized industry segment in sports. Professional teams include all of the various sports teams, leagues, and governing bodies for which individuals are paid for their performance. Some of the most notable organizations include the National Football League, National Basketball Association, National Hockey League, and Major League Baseball. These are commonly known as the four majors. During recent decades, more professional leagues have started, such as the Women's National Basketball Association, the Arena Football League, and Major League Soccer. There are also many minor league and collegiate organizations.

THE JOB

The two top positions in most sports organizations are *team president* and *general manager*. Depending on the size of the franchise, these two positions might be blended together and held by one person.

Team presidents are the chief executive officers of the club. They are responsible for the overall financial success of the team. Presidents oversee several departments within the organization, including marketing, public relations, broadcasting, sales, advertising, ticket sales, community relations, and accounting. Since team presidents must develop strategies to encourage fans to attend games, it is good if they have some experience in public relations or marketing. Along with the public relations manager, team presidents create give-away programs, such as cap days or poster nights.

Another one of the team president's responsibilities is encouraging community relations by courting season ticket holders, as well as those who purchase luxury box seats, known as skyboxes. Usually, this involves selling these seats to corporations.

General managers handle the daily business activities of the teams, such as hiring and firing, promotions, supervising scouting, making trades, and negotiating player contracts. All sports teams have general managers, and usually the main functions of the job are the same regardless of the team's professional level. However, some general managers that work with minor league teams might also deal with additional job duties, including managing the souvenir booths or organizing the ticket offices. The most important asset the general manager brings to an organization is knowledge of business practices.

REQUIREMENTS

High School
High school courses that will help you to become a sports executive include business, mathematics, and computer science. English, speech, and physical education courses will also be beneficial. Managing a school club or other organization will give you a general idea of the responsibilities and demands that this career involves.

Postsecondary Training
To become a sports executive, you will need at least a bachelor's degree. Remember, even though this is a sport-related position, presidents and general managers are expected to have the same backgrounds as corporate executives. Most have master's degrees in sports administration, and some have master's degrees in business administration.

Other Requirements
Sports executives must create a positive image for their teams. In this age of extensive media coverage (including the frequent public

speaking engagements that are required of sports executives), excellent communications skills are necessary. Sports executives need to be dynamic public speakers. They also need a keen business sense and an intimate knowledge of how to forge a good relationship with their communities. They also should have excellent organizational skills, be detail oriented, and be sound decision-makers.

EXPLORING

One way to start exploring this field is to volunteer to do something for your school's sports teams, for example, chart statistics or take on the duties of equipment manager. This is a way to begin learning how athletic departments work. Talk to the general manager of your local minor league baseball club, and try to get a part-time job with the team during the summer. When you are in college, try to get an internship within the athletic department to supplement your course of study. Any experience you gain in any area of sports administration will be valuable to you in your career as a sports executive. You may also find it helpful to read publications such as *Sports Business Journal* (http://www.sportsbusinessjournal.com).

EMPLOYERS

Employers include professional, collegiate, and minor-league football, hockey, baseball, basketball, soccer, and other sports teams. They are located across the United States and the world. About 6 percent of all athletes, coaches, and sports officials and related workers are employed in the commercial sports industry.

STARTING OUT

A majority of all sports executives begin their careers as interns. Interning offers the opportunity to gain recognition in an otherwise extremely competitive industry. Internships vary in length and generally include college credits. They are available in hundreds of sports categories and are offered by more than 90 percent of sports organizations. If you are serious about working in the sports industry, an internship is the most effective method of achieving your goals.

Entry-level positions in the sports industry are generally reserved for individuals with intern or volunteer experience. Once you have obtained this experience, you are eligible for thousands of entry-level positions in hundreds of fields. Qualified employees are hard to find in any industry, so the experience you have gained through internships will prove invaluable at this stage of your career.

Red Sox executives at a press conference announcing a trade that acquired pitcher Curt Shilling from the Arizona Diamondbacks. *(Jeff Topping, Reuters/Corbis)*

ADVANCEMENT

The experience prerequisite to qualify for a management-level position is generally three to five years in a specific field within the sports industry. At this level, an applicant should have experience managing a small to medium-sized staff and possess specific skills, including marketing, public relations, broadcasting, sales, advertising, publications, sports medicine, licensing, and specific sport player development.

The minimum experience to qualify for an executive position is generally seven years. Executives with proven records of accomplishment in the minors can be promoted to positions in the majors. Major league executives might receive promotions in the form of job offers from more prestigious teams.

EARNINGS

General managers, team presidents, and other sports executives earn salaries that range from $20,000 to $50,000 per year in the minor leagues to more than $1 million in the majors. Most sports executives are eligible for typical fringe benefits including medical and dental insurance, paid sick days and vacation time, and access to retirement savings plans.

WORK ENVIRONMENT

Sports team management is a fickle industry. When a team is winning, everyone loves the general manager or team president. When the team is losing, fans and the media often take out their frustrations on the team's executives. Sports executives must be able to handle that pressure. This industry is extremely competitive, and executives might find themselves without a job several times in their careers. Sports executives sleep, eat, and breathe their jobs, and definitely love the sports they manage.

OUTLOOK

The U.S. Department of Labor predicts that employment in amusement and recreation services (a category that includes sports-related careers) will grow faster than the average for all industries through 2016.

Although there are more sports executive positions available due to league expansion and the creation of new leagues, such as the Women's National Basketball Association, there still remain only a limited number of positions, and the competition for these jobs is very fierce. Being a sports executive demands both above-average business and leadership skills, in addition to a solid understanding of the demands and intricacies of a professional sports team. Those who obtain these jobs usually do so after many years of hard work. For that same reason, the rate of turnover in this field is low.

FOR MORE INFORMATION

Visit the society's Web site for information on membership for college students and a list of colleges and universities that offer sports management programs.
North American Society for Sport Management
http://www.nassm.com

To learn more about sports executive careers, contact
Teamwork Online LLC
Tel: 216-360-1790
Email: info@teamworkonline.com
http://www.teamworkonline.com

Sports Facility
Managers

QUICK FACTS

School Subjects
Business
English

Personal Skills
Leadership/management

Work Environment
Indoors and outdoors
Primarily one location

Minimum Education Level
Bachelor's degree

Salary Range
$34,970 to $67,690 to
$117,610+

Certification or Licensing
Recommended

Outlook
About as fast as the average

DOT
N/A

GOE
N/A

NOC
0721

O*NET
11-3011.00

OVERVIEW

Stadium, arena, and facility managers, sometimes called general managers, sports facility managers, or stadium operations executives, are responsible for the day-to-day operations involved in running a sports facility. They are involved in sports facility planning, including the buying, selling, or leasing of facilities; facility redesign and construction; and the supervision of sports facilities, including the structures and grounds, as well as the custodial crews.

HISTORY

Today's stadiums or arenas provide much more than a playing field and seats for sports and event spectators. The modern sports facility usually has one or more of the following: practice areas, home and visiting team locker rooms, physical therapy areas, sports equipment storage, press rooms, press boxes, facility maintenance equipment storage, cafeterias, and food vendor areas. It also normally includes offices for those who manage the facility, administer and assist the teams that play there, and promote and market the facility and the team. Those who manage these venues for sports events are responsible for ensuring that everything runs smoothly for the athletes, the fans, the advertisers, the media, and their own staff.

THE JOB

Stadium, arena, and facility managers are responsible for the day-to-day operations involved in running a sports facility. In the simplest terms, the manager of a sports facility, like other facility managers, must coordinate the events that occur in the facility with the services and people who make those events possible.

Sports facility managers are involved in sports facility planning, including the buying, selling, or leasing of facilities; facility redesign and construction; and the supervision of sports facilities, including the structures and grounds, as well as the custodial crews. This may mean months, sometimes even years, of research and long-term planning. Crucial resources and issues the manager might investigate include: sports facility design firms; prospective sites for the new facility and analyses of neighborhood support for a facility; and zoning laws or other federal, state, and local regulations concerning the construction of new buildings. Politics can play a key part in this process; the manager might be involved in these political meetings, as well. Once ground is broken on the new site, a sports facility manager may then divide his or her time between the construction site and the existing site, supervising both facilities until the new one is completed.

The manager of a sports facility, stadium, or arena who is not involved in the construction of a new facility, or the redesign of an existing one, spends most of his or her time in the office or somewhere in the facility itself, supervising the day-to-day management of the facility. The manager usually determines the organizational structure of the facility and establishes the personnel staffing requirements; setting up the manner in which things will be done and by whom. The facility manager is constantly analyzing how many different workers are needed to run the various areas of the facility efficiently, without sacrificing quality. The manager addresses staffing needs as they arise, setting the education, experience, and performance standards for each position. Depending on the size of the facility and the nature of the manager's assigned responsibilities, this may mean hiring a personnel director to screen prospective employees, or it may mean the manager personally sifts through stacks of resumes whenever a position opens up. Usually, all policies and procedures having to do with the morale, safety, service, appearance, and performance of facility employees (and which are not determined by the organization, itself) are determined by the manager.

The manager of a sports facility is also responsible for assisting with the development and coordination of the facility's annual operating calendar, including activity schedules, dates and hours of operation, and projections for attendance and revenue. Often, a manager for a sports facility directs and assists with the procurement of activities and events to take place at the facility; this, of course, depends on the size of the facility. A large, multipurpose stadium, for example, will probably have at least one individual devoted to event planning and the acquisition of activities. Even in this case, however, the sports facility manager must be involved in coordinating the event with all the other aspects of the facility.

The sports facility manager handles the negotiations, contracts, and agreements with industry agents, suppliers, and vendors. These days, many jobs that used to be handled in-house by staff employees are now contracted out to private companies that specialize in that aspect of the event. Food service and security, for example, are two areas that usually are privately managed by outside vendors and firms. It is the responsibility of the sports facility manager to hire such contractors and to monitor the quality of their work.

Finally, it is the manager's duty to make certain that the facility, its workers, and the services it offers are in accordance with federal, state, and local regulations.

Although certain responsibilities are shared, the job description for a sports facility manager will inevitably vary according to the type of sport played and the level of the organization that employs the manager. For example, the duties of a manager for a parks and recreation facility in a medium-sized town will differ considerably from those of the general manager of Churchill Downs in Louisville, Kentucky; the former will do many of the duties that the latter would most likely delegate to others.

The type of sports stadium, arena, or auditorium in which sports facility managers work also varies, from racetracks to natatoriums to large, multipurpose stadiums that host football games and rock concerts.

REQUIREMENTS

High School

High school courses that will give you a general background for work in sports facility management include business, mathematics, government, and computer science. Speech and writing classes will help you to hone your communication skills. Managing a school club or other organization will introduce you to overseeing budgets and the work of others.

Postsecondary Training

These days, a bachelor's degree is pretty much required to enter the field of sports facility management. Although in the past it wasn't necessary, the competition for jobs in sports administration and facility management is so keen that a bachelor's degree is nearly mandatory. In fact, in many instances, a master's degree in sports administration or sports facility management is increasingly required of managers.

The oldest program in the country in sports administration and facility management is at Ohio University in Athens, Ohio. Administered by the School of Recreation and Sports Sciences within Ohio University's College of Health and Human Services, the program requires 55 credit hours (five of which are completed during an internship) and leads to the master of sports administration degree. The curriculum focuses on business administration, journalism, communications, management, marketing, sports administration, and facility management. The required internship lasts anywhere from three months to a year and internship opportunities are provided by more than 400 different organizations worldwide. (See "For More Information" at the end of this article for contact information for this program.)

Certification or Licensing

At the moment, certification in facility management is not mandatory, but it is becoming a distinguishing credential among the managers of the largest, most profitable venues. A sports stadium or arena brings its owners a lot of revenue, and these owners aren't willing to trust the management of such lucrative venues to individuals who are not qualified to run them; certification is one way an administration can ensure that certain industry standards in facility management are met. The International Facility Management Association, probably the industry leader in certification, offers the designation of certified facility manager. The International Association of Assembly Managers also offers the certification designation of certified facilities executive. For contact information for these associations, see the end of this article.

Other Requirements

Most organizations want their facility managers to have, at a minimum, five years of experience in the field or industry. This may include participation in a sport at the professional level, marketing or promotions work, or related management experience that can be shown as relevant to the responsibilities and duties of a sports facility manager.

Leadership and communication skills are considered essential to be successful in this career. In the course of an average day, you might review designs for a new stadium with top-level executives, release a statement to members of the press about the groundbreaking ceremony for the new stadium, and interview prospective supervisors for maintenance work. You will need to be able to state clearly and concisely your ideas, information, and goals, regardless of the audience.

Finally, you should possess excellent strategic, budgetary, and operational planning skills; the day-to-day operations of the sports facility will run on the decisions that you make, so you need to be capable of juggling many different tasks.

EXPLORING

If you aren't actively involved with a sport as a participant, you can get involved with sports administration and management by volunteering for positions with your own high school teams. Any and all experience helps, beginning with organizing and managing the equipment for a football team, for example, all the way up to working as a team statistician. You can also work with their local booster club to sponsor events that promote athletics within the school district. These activities demonstrate your interest and devotion and may help you in the future by providing you with an edge when searching for an internship.

Part-time or summer jobs as ushers, vendors, ball boys or girls, for example, not only provide firsthand experience for both high school and college students, but also can lead to other contacts and opportunities.

College students interested in sports facility management can often locate valuable internships through contacts they have developed from part-time jobs, but the placement centers in undergraduate or graduate programs in business administration and facility management are also good places to consult for information on internships. The professional leagues and associations for specific sports—the National Hockey League, the National Football League, and the National Basketball Association, for example—all offer summer internships. Competition for positions with these organizations is extremely keen, so interested students should send for application materials well in advance, study them, and apply early.

Professional organizations within the field also sponsor opportunities to learn on the job. The International Association of Assembly Managers (IAAM) offers internships to qualified students. Typically, participating facilities that serve as sites for IAAM internships are responsible for the selection of their interns. While some of these facilities aren't specifically geared toward sporting events, much of the management skills and responsibilities are shared and will provide you with a wonderful opportunity to learn firsthand.

EMPLOYERS

Sports facility managers may work for a single team, a multisports arena or stadium, or they may work for a city or state organization, such as a parks and recreation department.

STARTING OUT

Graduates of programs in sports administration and sports facility management usually find jobs through internships they have had, personal contacts they developed in the field, or from job listings in their graduate programs' placement departments.

Entry-level jobs may be in facility management, or they may come in a related field. Most organizations like to promote from within, so it isn't uncommon for someone with a bachelor's or graduate degree in facility management who is working in, for example, public relations, to be considered first for an opening in the sports facility department. Associate- or assistant-level positions are the most likely entry point for graduates, but those with exceptional education and experience may qualify for managerial positions after graduation, although this is rare. In fact, as the field becomes more popular, it will be increasingly difficult to enter a sports facility management position without a bachelor's degree and a solid internship experience, at the very least.

Those who find entry-level jobs are helped by mentors. Mentoring is an industry-supported method in which an older, experienced member of a facility management team helps a younger, less-experienced individual to learn the ropes. This process helps the person learn and aids the organization by reducing problems caused by inexperienced beginners.

ADVANCEMENT

Experience and certification are the best ways for someone to advance in this field. Years of successful on-the-job experience count for a great deal in this industry; the owners and administrations of professional teams and sports venues look for someone who has demonstrated the ability to make things run smoothly. Certification is becoming another way in which success can be gauged; more and more frequently, certification garners salary increases and promotions for those who hold it. Increasingly, firms are asking for certified facility managers when they begin job searches. Since certification goes hand-in-hand with experience, it is assumed that those individuals who are certified are the best in their field.

Outside of experience and certification, a willingness and eagerness to learn and branch into new areas is a less objective manner for gauging which managers will land top jobs. Those who are willing to embrace new technology and are open to new ideas and methods for improving efficiency will very likely advance in their careers.

Advancement might also mean changing specialties or developing one. Sports facility managers who are interested in other areas of management may decide to leave the field and involve themselves with different venues, such as auditoriums, performing arts centers, or convention centers, to name just a few. Still others might advance to manage international venues.

EARNINGS

Earnings for sports facility managers vary considerably depending on their experience and education, as well as the level of the facility that employs them. Administrative services managers (the category under which the U.S. Department of Labor classifies sports facility managers) earned median annual salaries of $67,690 in 2006. The lowest paid 10 percent earned less than $34,970, and the highest paid 10 percent earned $117,610 or more per year. Facility managers who are certified earn higher salaries than those who are not certified. The International Facility Management Association reports that members who held the certified facility manager designation earned an average of 13 percent more than their non-certified counterparts.

WORK ENVIRONMENT

One of the perks of the profession is the glamorous atmosphere that the job promotes; sports facility managers work to provide a unique environment for amateur and professional athletes, sometimes even celebrities and other performers. Although their work most often is behind-the-scenes, they may have indirect or direct contact with the high-profile personalities who perform in large venues. Sports facility managers usually work in clean, comfortable offices. Since their work often involves other activities, such as construction, they also may spend a great deal of time at construction sites and in trailers, supervising the construction of a new facility.

The management of a sports arena or stadium naturally involves promotional events, both for the building and the teams or events that are staged there. To be successful in their work, facility managers must maintain regular contact with the members of other departments, such as marketing and public relations.

A sports facility manager's job can be stressful. Construction, renovation, and cleaning and maintenance deadlines must all be met in order to ensure the efficient operation of a sports facility, let alone one in which major sports events occur. Depending on the level of the facility and the nature of events that are staged there, the responsibilities of the manager often require more hours on the job than the typical nine-to-five day allows. Additional work may be necessary, but is often uncompensated.

OUTLOOK

In general, the future for facilities managers is much brighter than it is for those in other administrative services. This relatively young field is growing quickly. Moreover, the profession is not as subject to cost-cutting pressures, especially in the private sector, or as vulnerable to government cutbacks. Demand for jobs in sports administration is great, and the newer field of sports facility management is quickly catching up.

FOR MORE INFORMATION

For certification information, job listings, student chapters, internships, and to subscribe to Facility Manager, *contact*
International Association of Assembly Managers
635 Fritz Drive, Suite 100
Coppell, TX 75019-4442
Tel: 972-906-7441
http://www.iaam.org

For information on certification and to subscribe to Facility Management Journal, *contact*
International Facility Management Association
1 East Greenway Plaza, Suite 1100
Houston, TX 77046-0194
Tel: 713-623-4362
Email: ifma@ifma.org
http://www.ifma.org

For information on the master of sports administration degree, contact

Sports Administration/Facility Management Program
Ohio University
School of Recreation and Sport Sciences
E148 Grover Center
Athens, OH 45701-2979
Tel: 740-593-4666
Email: sportsad@ohiou.edu
http://www.sportsad.ohio.edu

For industry information, contact
Stadium Managers Association
525 SW 5th Street, Suite A
Des Moines, IA 50309-4501
Tel: 515-282-8192
Email: sma@assoc-mgmt.com
http://www.stadiummanagers.org

Supermarket Managers

OVERVIEW

Supermarket managers work in grocery stores. They manage budgets, arrange schedules, oversee human resources, lead customer service, and manage each aspect of the day-to-day business of bringing the nation's food supply to the people.

Managers include store managers, assistant store managers, courtesy booth/service desk managers, customer service managers, receiving managers, and managers of such departments as bakery, deli/food service, food court, front end, grocery, meat/seafood, frozen foods, pharmacy, and produce/floral. The size and location of the store determines how many of these management levels exist in each store. In a small, family-owned grocery, the manager and owner may be the same person. There are 3.4 million food store employees in the United States.

HISTORY

In the early 1900s, the supermarket "industry," was really a group of small "mom and pop" grocery stores. At most of these stores, the owners or members of their family managed the daily operations. The typical city street of that time resembled the supermarket departments of today, with each store handling its own specialty. For example, the fish market and the bakery each had an individual owner and operator.

By 1902, Kroger, now the country's largest grocer (by number of stores), already had 40 stores and a factory as well as a management staff to keep the growing business efficient. As Americans began purchasing more of their food and relying less on their gardens and farms, the supermarket industry grew along with the need for professionals to manage the stores.

Technological innovations have increased the duties and responsibilities of supermarket managers. Bar codes, inventory systems, and complex delivery systems have increased the need for professionals who can use these tools to run an efficient store while still remembering that customer service is of utmost importance. With profit margins low and competition high in this $499.5 billion industry (in 2006), careful business planning is imperative for each store's success.

At the beginning of the century, locally owned groceries were the norm, although some chains were already growing. However, that has changed with the rapid growth of chain supermarkets. While chains have purchased some local stores and companies, other small stores have simply gone out of business.

Advances in technology will continue to alter the duties of the supermarket manager. Online grocery shopping is predicted to grow rapidly over the next few years. Qualified managers trained in the newest technology and management practices will be needed in this evolving industry.

THE JOB

Supermarket managers oversee a wide range of resources, both personal and professional, to do their jobs effectively. Their days are fast paced and interesting; routine duties are often interspersed with the need to solve problems quickly and effectively.

Steve Edens is the associate manager of a Kroger supermarket in Columbus, Indiana. Like most supermarket managers, Edens works a variety of shifts and handles a range of responsibilities. Working as the liaison between the corporate office and his staff, Edens spends time each day handling correspondence, email, and verbal and written reports.

Supermarket managers often work on more than one task at once. Edens carries a note pad and a scan gun, and he pushes a cart as he checks the floor, inventory, and departments each day. While checking the inventory, Edens uses the scan gun to check on an item that is low in stock. The scan gun lets him know if the item has been ordered. "The technology keeps getting better and better," says Edens. The average supermarket carries 45,000 different items, so the technology of today helps managers to keep those items on the shelves.

You may think that managers rarely get their hands dirty, but this is not the case for Edens and other managers. Edens carries a feather duster with him as he makes his daily rounds of the store. Appearance is crucial for a supermarket's image as well as maintaining customer comfort, so Edens occasionally straightens and dusts as he surveys the placement of advertising material, merchandise, and other store features. The typical supermarket covers 48,750 square feet, so managers must be prepared to spend a lot of time each day walking.

Planning is key for supermarket managers. They must prepare weekly schedules, which are carefully coordinated with the wage budget. The managers work with the head cashier to check and coordinate schedules. The manager and associate manager oversee a staff of department heads that vary with the size and location of the store.

These department and subdepartment managers are in charge of specific areas of the store, such as the bakery and deli, frozen foods, or produce. The department managers, along with the store managers, interview prospective employees, while the store managers do the actual hiring and firing of personnel. Large supermarkets may employ more than 250 people, so supermarket managers need to have good human resources training.

Department heads also handle specific promotions within their areas as well as customer service within those areas. Many store managers have worked previously as department managers.

Promotion and advertising are also on the managers' list of responsibilities. "We always plan a week ahead on displays and sales," says Edens, noting that seasonal displays are as important in the grocery industry as in any other retail industry.

One of the major responsibilities of each of the managers is customer service. Managers need to courteously and competently address the requests and complaints of store customers. "I like working with people," says Edens. "It's very satisfying to me when I can help a customer out."

Edens acknowledges that the compensation—both monetarily and personally—is high, but he has worked many 60- to 70-hour weeks and most holidays. "I don't think I've ever had an entire three-day weekend off," says Edens. "You work most holidays." Many stores are open 24 hours a day, seven days a week, and 365 days a year. With at least two managers required to be on duty at a time, supermarket managers can expect to work late nights, weekends, and holidays.

A manager trainee arranges products in the organic foods section at a supermarket. *(Dick Blume, Syracuse Newspapers/The Image Works)*

At larger stores, such as the Columbus Kroger, scheduling is often easier and requires fewer hours from each manager, since the load can be split up among a larger management staff. Managers at smaller stores should expect to work more hours, weekends, and holidays.

Frequent transfers are also common. Edens has worked at over 10 stores during his 24-year career. Although his transfers have not involved household moves, larger companies do pay moving expenses for management transfers.

Problem solving and quick thinking are key skills to being a successful supermarket manager. Delayed deliveries, snowstorms, or holidays can throw a wrench into schedules, inventory, and effective customer service. Managers need to deal with these problems as they happen while still preparing for the next day, week, and month.

REQUIREMENTS

High School

Speech classes will help you build your communication skills, while business and mathematics courses will give you a good background for preparing budgets. Because reading is integral in evaluating reports and communicating with others, English classes are required for workers in this field. Any specific classes in marketing, advertising, or statistics will also be helpful. Learning how to work well with others is important, so any classes that involve group projects or participation will help you to develop teamwork skills.

Postsecondary Training

While a college degree is not required for a career in supermarket management, there is a trend toward hiring new managers straight out of college. Even for college-educated managers, stores have their own specific training programs, which may involve classes, on-site learning, and rotational training in different departments.

Some colleges offer degrees in retail management, but many people choose to major in business management to prepare for a management career. Even an associate's degree in retail or business management will give you an advantage over applicants who have only a high school diploma.

Other Requirements

Interacting with people and handling customer service is the biggest requirement of the job. According to the Food Marketing Institute, the average consumer makes 1.9 trips to the grocery store per week. With this many people in each store, serving those people with professionalism and courtesy should be the number one goal of supermarket managers.

To be a supermarket manager, you should be able to handle a fast-paced and challenging work environment and have the ability to calmly solve unexpected and frequent problems. Besides being able to "think on your feet," you should be able to evaluate analytical problems with budgets, schedules, and promotions.

EXPLORING

If you are interested in becoming a supermarket manager, get a job at a supermarket. Any job, from bagger to cashier, will help you understand the industry better. Supermarket jobs are readily available to students, and the opportunity for on-the-job experience is great.

Interview managers to discuss the things they like and do not like about their jobs. Ask these managers how they got started and what influenced them to choose this career. When you set up your interview, be sensitive to seasonal and weather concerns. Supermarket managers are extremely busy during holidays or other times when people flock to the stores in droves.

Look ahead. Online shopping is just one of the new trends in supermarkets. Be aware of industry innovations, and evaluate how your skills might fit into this changing industry.

Take some business classes and join or start a business club at your school. If you love people, but can't create a budget, this is not the career for you.

Hang out at your local store. Go on a busy day and a slow one. Study what activities are taking place and how management's role changes from day to day. Get a feel for the pace to decide if you would want to spend many hours in a retail atmosphere.

EMPLOYERS

Kroger is the largest supermarket chain and employer (by number of stores) in the United States, operating over 3,250 food and convenience stores in 2006. Supervalu Inc. (2,531 stores), Wal-Mart Supercenters (2,195), Safeway (1,767), and Delhaize America (1,529) round out the top five chains.

Over the past 10 years, the number of chain supermarkets has grown while the number of small, independent grocers has decreased. While this makes the number of stores and employers smaller, the larger stores need a variety of management professionals for a diverse number of positions, from department managers to store managers.

Grocery stores are located in nearly every city. Smaller cities and towns may have only one or two supermarkets to choose from, but consumers and prospective employees in larger cities have a wide selection of chains and smaller stores. More than 34,019 supermarkets in the United States report annual sales of at least $2 million, and approximately 3.4 million people in the U.S. are employed at food stores.

STARTING OUT

You won't be able to start out as a supermarket manager; some experience is usually necessary before assuming a managerial role. You can start as a bagger or cashier or as a management trainee. There are two basic career paths—either working through the ranks or being hired after completing a college program. Steve Edens started in the stock room and has worked in a variety of positions from cashier to department manager and now as an associate manager. Working in many areas of the store is an important part of becoming an effective manager.

Supermarket Facts, 2006

Total supermarket sales:	$499.5 billion
Average sale per customer transaction:	$29.26
Average number of customer trips per week:	1.9
Average number of items carried in a supermarket:	45,000
Median average store size in square feet:	48,750

Sources: Food Marketing Institute, U.S. Department of Agriculture

"This is one of the few companies where you can start as a bag boy and become the president," says Edens. Hard work and dedication are rewarded, so paying your dues is important in this career.

To be considered for a management position, grocery experience is necessary. Even other retail experience is not enough to be hired as a manager because the grocery industry has so many specific challenges that are unique to the field.

Cold call applications are readily accepted at customer service counters in most grocery stores, and larger grocers conduct on-campus recruiting to attract future managers. Newspaper advertisements are also used to recruit new workers for this field.

ADVANCEMENT

Department managers can advance up the management ladder to store manager or associate store manager. After reaching that level, the next step in advancement is to the corporate level—becoming a unit, district, or regional manager, responsible for a number of stores. The next step at the corporate level is to vice president or director of store operations. Managers at the store level can advance and receive higher salaries by transferring to larger and higher-earning stores. Some relocations may require a move to another city, state, or region, while others simply require a bit longer or shorter commute.

EARNINGS

Supermarket managers are well compensated. According to the U.S. Department of Labor, first-line supervisors/managers of retail workers averaged $33,960 in 2006. Salaries ranged from less than $21,420 to $59,710 or more annually. Department managers at large stores average $75,000 annually. District managers earn average salaries of $100,000 annually. These salary numbers may include bonuses that are standard in the industry. Pay is affected by management level, the size of the store, and the location.

Benefits are also good, with most major employers offering health insurance, vacation pay, and sick pay. While some supermarket workers are covered by a union, managers are not required to pay union dues and do not receive overtime pay.

WORK ENVIRONMENT

Supermarkets are clean and brightly lit. Depending on the time of day, they may be noisy or quiet, crowded or empty. Nearly all supermarket work takes place indoors, and most managers will spend several hours on their feet walking through the store while also spending time at an office desk.

A team environment pervades the supermarket, and managers are the head of that team. They must work well independently while supervising and communicating with others.

Supermarket managers are expected to work more than 40-hour weeks and also work holidays, weekends, and late hours. Because many supermarkets are open 24 hours a day, rotating schedules are usually required. In addition, calls at home and last-minute schedule changes are to be expected.

OUTLOOK

Managers in the supermarket industry should expect growth that is slower than the average for all occupations. While the number of stores (and managers needed to run them) is decreasing, specialization and demand will create demand for the best-trained and most knowledgeable managers. "There is a big demand for qualified people," says Steve Edens. "Supermarkets need people with experience and good people skills." This growth in grocery management is due to an expanding line of inventory and specialization. Because there is strong competition in the supermarket industry, stores are creating new departments, such as restaurants, coffee shops, and movie rental departments, to meet consumers' needs.

With total supermarket sales of $499.5 billion in 2006, the industry is huge and continues to grow as consumers spend more money on greater varieties of food and other merchandise. There will be demand for people who can manage others while mastering the latest technology. Grocery stores are often at the forefront in exploring new technologies to improve efficiency, so computer literacy and business acumen will be increasingly important.

FOR MORE INFORMATION

For industry and employment information, contact
Food Marketing Institute
2345 Crystal Drive, Suite 800
Arlington, VA 22202-4813
Tel: 202-452-8444
http://www.fmi.org

For general information on retail fields, contact
National Retail Federation
325 7th Street, NW, Suite 1100
Washington, DC 20004-2818
Tel: 800-673-4692
http://www.nrf.com

For information on jobs in retail, contact
Retail Industry Leaders Association
1700 North Moore Street, Suite 2250
Arlington, VA 22209-1933
Tel: 703-841-2300
http://www.retail-leaders.org

Index